T0068150

LORD JESUS, PLEASE HELP ME FIND MY HAPPY

DAVID BOUDREAUX

WESTBOW
PRESS®
A DIVISION OF THOMAS NELSON
& ZONDERVAN

Copyright © 2022 David Boudreaux.

All rights reserved. No part of this book may be used or reproduced by
any means, graphic, electronic, or mechanical, including photocopying,
recording, taping or by any information storage retrieval system
without the written permission of the author except in the case of
brief quotations embodied in critical articles and reviews.

This book is a work of non-fiction. Unless otherwise noted, the author
and the publisher make no explicit guarantees as to the accuracy of
the information contained in this book and in some cases, names of
people and places have been altered to protect their privacy.

WestBow Press books may be ordered through booksellers or by contacting:

WestBow Press
A Division of Thomas Nelson & Zondervan
1663 Liberty Drive
Bloomington, IN 47403
www.westbowpress.com
844-714-3454

Because of the dynamic nature of the Internet, any web addresses or
links contained in this book may have changed since publication and
may no longer be valid. The views expressed in this work are solely those
of the author and do not necessarily reflect the views of the publisher,
and the publisher hereby disclaims any responsibility for them.

Any people depicted in stock imagery provided by Getty Images are
models, and such images are being used for illustrative purposes only.
Certain stock imagery © Getty Images.

Scripture taken from the King James Version of the Bible.

ISBN: 978-1-6642-6101-3 (sc)
ISBN: 978-1-6642-6103-7 (hc)
ISBN: 978-1-6642-6102-0 (e)

Library of Congress Control Number: 2022904993

Print information available on the last page.

WestBow Press rev. date: 03/28/2022

CONTENTS

PREFACE

This work is a product of the Holy Spirit speaking to me concerning the way many Christians today do not appear to have much to be happy about. I understand life is full of problems, situations, and concerns that can steal your joy, but I don't believe this is how God expects us to live. From everything I have read and studied concerning God's people, we should be showing the world the joy, happiness, and contentment that comes from accepting Jesus Christ as our savior. Serving God should not be grievous but exciting and joyful. Following God's will for our lives should be fulfilling. Having faith in our God should bring peace and contentment. I believe there are several reasons why, to a large degree, this is not what we are witnessing among Christians. Partly it may be because not everyone who says they are Christians are really saved. Partly it is because many true believers have not found or surrendered to God's will. Partly it may be due to the fact that they have not learned to accept that whatever God brings into their lives as part of God's will for them. I believe one of the main reasons is that people have set their eyes on the things of the earth instead of on the things of heaven and therefore have lost their first love. Through the guidance of the Holy Spirit, I wanted to help Christians refocus on God and restore their joy in Christ Jesus. You can have the peace of God that passes all understanding, so let me help you find your way.

CHAPTER 1

Obstacles to My Happy

I see so many Christian people walking around looking like someone licked all the red off their candy. That is an expression my dad used when he saw us kids in a bad mood. He also used to say, "You look like you've been sucking on a green persimmon." I don't know if any of you have ever sucked on a green persimmon, but if you have, then that one needs no explanation. They were so sour that they would make your whole face pucker up. I can understand why some people would be in a bad mood all the time, but with Christians I don't believe this should be so.

I spent a considerable amount of time just thinking about what makes people unhappy—all people, not just Christians—and this is what came up randomly. People are unhappy because of fear, worry, or doubt. They are unhappy because of indecisiveness, uncertainty, or the unknown. Sometimes people are unhappy because of envy, strife, jealousy, or shame. Some are unhappy because of weakness, helplessness, discouragement, and suspicion. Others are unhappy because of their unforgiveness, grudges, anxiety, or hopelessness, and others because they lack direction or purpose in their lives. Some are unhappy because they lack self-worth, confidence, or trust in others around them. Some are unhappy because of the fear of failure or perhaps the lack of sufficient accomplishment. Some are probably not happy because of pride, confusion, or frustration. Some are not happy because of disorder in their lives, lack of proper guidance, or lack of faith. They may not be happy because of unfulfilled desires, lies, deceit, or temptations, or perhaps because of judgment, self-righteousness, criticism, or self-reliance. They could be unhappy because of stress, lack of humility, boastfulness, anger, wrath, and malice. Maybe they're unhappy because of physical limitations, failure to set personal goals, or the inability to meet those goals. They could lack personal values or morals or experience confusion, uncertainty, or insecurity concerning their future. Some are unhappy because they put their faith in men or women instead of God and they ended up being disappointed or hurt. Some people are unhappy because they don't know what God wants from them and they do not have their priorities right concerning their lives or their families.

Some of these things I continued to experience as an immature Christian, but mostly these are issues I was familiar with as a non-Christian. For me to describe adequately how you should deal with all these issues in your life as a Christian, we must first ensure that you have been saved and that you have the tools needed to defeat these fiery darts from the devil. I will tell you from the get-go, as they say, that unless you are a born-again Christian, you do not have the tools needed to defeat the devil.

The first thing needed in order to win the war over unhappiness or depression is to accept God's plan for your life. This plan includes you having the opportunity to hear the gospel (i.e., the plan of salvation) and either accept Christ as your savior or denying him.

This is God's plan for your salvation.

The first step toward salvation from the destiny of eternal separation from God in a place called hell is to realize that you need to be saved. We need a savior because we are all sinners and fall short of the glory of God.

As it is written, There is none righteous, no, not one. (Romans 3:10)

They are all gone out of the way, they are together become unprofitable; there is none that doeth good, no, not one. (Romans 3:12)

Whose mouth is full of cursing and bitterness. (Romans 3:14)

Now we know that what things soever the law saith, it saith to them who are under the law: that every mouth may be stopped, and all the world may become guilty before God. Therefore by the deeds of the law there shall no flesh be justified in his sight: for by the law is the knowledge of sin. (Romans 3:19–20)

For all have sinned, and come short of the glory of God. (Romans 3:23)

You may think you are a good person and you are not guilty of any sin bad enough to send you to hell. What you need to see is that which sins you are guilty of is irrelevant. The sin is disobeying God's laws, and everyone is guilty of that. This makes sins without degree; they are all equal in the fact that we disobeyed God. Because of this, no one is innocent; we are all guilty before God. Allow me to illustrate. How many lies does a person have to tell before he or she is guilty of being a liar? How many sins must one commit before that person is guilty of being a sinner? I think we all know the answer. So how many sins must you commit before you are guilty before God of breaking his laws? We need to realize we were already guilty. Jesus did not come to make us guilty of sin; we did that on our own. There are those who would tell you that you can earn your way to heaven by doing good works, or in other words by keeping God's laws. If it were possible to keep all of God's laws, then that would be true, but it isn't possible. The problem is that humans are not capable of keeping God's laws, and that is why God gave us the law: so we would be able to see our guilt. If we could keep all the laws, we wouldn't need a savior. This would be salvation by good works. The Bible tells us this is not possible.

> For by grace are ye saved through faith; and that not of yourselves: it is the gift of God. Not of works, lest any man should boast. (Ephesians 2:8–9)

The Bible also teaches us that the wages (i.e., what we deserve to pay) for being sinners is death.

> For the wages of sin is death; but the gift of God is eternal life through Jesus Christ our Lord. (Romans 6:23)

The word *death* here means "to separate" or "to take away." In this case, it refers to the separation of your spirit from the presence of God for all eternity. The laws of God were given to humankind in order to make us realize we needed to be saved from ourselves because of what we have done. This same verse, however, also declares that there remains a glimmer of hope for humankind. That is because God is willing to give us a gift. This gift that he is offering is eternal life through his son Jesus Christ. Humans do not have the ability to save themselves, but God has a plan for their salvation. This salvation is a gift from God and cannot be earned by any man or woman. Don't try to blame God for the human condition. He has done everything possible to save us.

> For God sent not his Son into the world to condemn the world; but that the world through him might be

saved. He that believeth on him is not condemned: but he that believeth not is condemned already, because he hath not believed in the name of the only begotten Son of God. (John 3:17–18)

After you realize you are a sinner and stand guilty before God, you must feel remorseful for your sins, or sorry that you were unable to remain sinless. This is repentance; without repentance, there is no remission of sins (i.e., without repentance sins cannot be forgiven).

For godly sorrow worketh repentance to salvation not to be repented of: but the sorrow of the world worketh death. (2Corinthians 7:10)

The Lord is not slack concerning his promise, as some men count slackness; but is longsuffering to us-ward, not willing that any should perish, but that all should come to repentance. (2Peter 3:9)

Repent ye therefore, and be converted, that your sins may be blotted out, when the times of refreshing shall come from the presence of the Lord. (Acts 3:19)

After you have repented, you are prepared to receive the gift of eternal life. This is accomplished by believing that Jesus is the Son of God and that he came here to earth from heaven to die on the cross in order to pay the price for your sins. This is obviously not the same as just believing that there is a God. It is believing that Jesus Christ is God and that He came here to save you. The devil believes in God and trembles with fear in God's presence.

> Thou believest that there is one God; thou doest well: the devils also believe, and tremble. (James 2:19)

Believing is faith, that is, believing that Jesus is who He claims to be and that He can do what He says he can do for you. When you repent of your sins and believe in Christ, all that remains is for you to ask Him to save you.

> That if thou shalt confess with thy mouth the Lord Jesus, and shalt believe in thine heart that God hath raised him from the dead, thou shalt be saved. For with the heart man believeth unto righteousness; and with the mouth confession is made unto salvation. For the scripture saith, Whosoever believeth on him shall not be ashamed. For there is no difference between the Jew and the Greek: for the same Lord over all is rich unto all that call upon him. For whosoever shall call upon the name of the Lord shall be saved. (Romans 10:9–13)

Faith must be exercised in order to mean anything. If I say I believe the old, broken-down fold-up lawn chair out in the backyard will hold me up if I sit on it, some may believe me and some may not. I may not even believe it myself; faith without action is empty. However, if I sit on that chair, then I have proven I have enough faith in the chair that I'm willing to trust it with my well-being. Then the faith means something. If you call on Jesus to save you then you must exercise your faith and believe in your heart that He did what you asked Him to do. When you put your faith in Christ there is no more condemnation. You are no longer guilty of being a sinner.

> But God commendeth his love toward us, in that,
> while we were yet sinners, Christ died for us.
> (Romans 5:8)

After you become a child of God through our Lord Jesus Christ, there is no power in heaven, in hell, or on earth that can change that.

> For I am persuaded, that neither death, nor life, nor
> angels, nor principalities, nor powers, nor things
> present, nor things to come, Nor height, nor depth,
> nor any other creature, shall be able to separate us
> from the love of God, which is in Christ Jesus our
> Lord. (Romans 8:38–39)

Unfortunately, there are those who would tell you that you can lose your salvation by not following or keeping Gods' laws. This doesn't make any sense to me. If there is no good work I can do that is good enough to save me in the first place, then how are good works going to keep me saved? I personally thank God my salvation doesn't depend on my ability to keep God's laws. I think I would lose my salvation in the first ten minutes of every day. Good works can't save you, and they can't keep you saved. As long as you have doubts about whether Jesus actually saved you like He said He would or that you may not be able to stay saved, it limits God's ability to use you to do his work while you are here on earth. It is God's will for every Christian to become mature in his or her spiritual life and to become a servant in His ministry. I would like to encourage anyone who has read this plan of salvation and has not already secured their place in heaven to do so right now. Even if you have gone through all the motions or said all the words before but you didn't really understand what you were doing at the time, then you should do it again. I don't believe you can be saved unless you understand what you are doing at the time. I say it is better to know for sure. If you were saved the first time, then you are just reaffirming your position with God, and if you're not sure then this will give you the assurance you need to move forward in your Christian life. Just say this simple prayer.

> Heavenly Father, I know that I am a sinner, and I cannot go to heaven with my sin. I am sorry for being a sinner, and I am coming to you asking for your forgiveness. I believe that Jesus Christ is your Son and that He is God and that you have the authority to forgive me. Lord, please forgive me for being a sinner and make me a born-again child of God. Lord, I do believe that you have done what I have asked you to do, and from this day forward I want to live a life that is pleasing to you. In Jesus' name I pray. Amen.

CHAPTER 2

Removing Obstacles

As I looked over the list of obstacles to happiness, it brought to mind some scriptures I need to share with you. These scriptures describe the works of the flesh. Even if you are a born-again Christian, you are still living in a corruptible body until your physical body dies and your spirit goes to heaven or until the rapture takes place and you receive your incorruptible body. The battle taking place inside you each day is between your earthly corruptible flesh and your spirit, which is now one with the spirit of God. Before you were saved, your spirit belonged to the devil because he is the ruler of this world. There was no war going on then between righteousness and unrighteousness because your spirit and your flesh both served the devil.

> Mortify therefore your members which are upon the earth; fornication, uncleanness, inordinate affection, evil concupiscence, and covetousness, which is idolatry For which things' sake the wrath of God cometh on the children of disobedience
>
> In the which ye also walked some time, when ye lived in them. But now ye also put off all these; anger, wrath, malice, blasphemy, filthy communication

out of your mouth. Lie not one to another, seeing
that ye have put off the old man with his deeds;
And have put on the new man, which is renewed in
knowledge after the image of him that created him.
(Colossians 3:5–10)

This I say then, Walk in the Spirit, and ye shall
not fulfil the lust of the flesh. For the flesh lusteth
against the Spirit, and the Spirit against the flesh:
and these are contrary the one to the other: so that
ye cannot do the things that ye would. But if ye be
led of the Spirit, ye are not under the law. Now the
works of the flesh are manifest, which are these;
Adultery, fornication, uncleanness, lasciviousness,
Idolatry, witchcraft, hatred, variance, emulations,
wrath, strife, seditions, heresies, Envyings, murders,
drunkenness, revellings, and such like: of the which
I tell you before, as I have also told you in time past,
that they which do such things shall not inherit
the kingdom of God. But the fruit of the Spirit is
love, joy, peace, longsuffering, gentleness, goodness,
faith, Meekness, temperance: against such there is
no law. And they that are Christ's have crucified
the flesh with the affections and lusts. (Galatians
5:16-24)

Be ye therefore followers of God, as dear children.
And walk in love, as Christ also hath loved us,
and hath given himself for us an offering and a
sacrifice to God for a sweet smelling savour. But
fornication, and all uncleanness, or covetousness,
let it not be once named among you, as becometh
saints; Neither filthiness, nor foolish talking, nor
jesting, which are not convenient: but rather giving

of thanks. For this ye know, that no whoremonger, nor unclean person, nor covetous man, who is an idolater, hath any inheritance in the kingdom of Christ and of God. Let no man deceive you with vain words: for because of these things cometh the wrath of God upon the children of disobedience. Be not ye therefore partakers with them. For ye were sometimes darkness, but now are ye light in the Lord: walk as children of light: (For the fruit of the Spirit is in all goodness and righteousness and truth;) Proving what is acceptable unto the Lord. And have no fellowship with the unfruitful works of darkness, but rather reprove them. For it is a shame even to speak of those things which are done of them in secret. (Ephesians 5:1-12)

In all these verses, we are reminded that these issues we have are issues of the flesh; in other words, they are works of the flesh. Do the lists of fleshly works in these verses not sound almost exactly like the list I showed you in the beginning of chapter one? I am not going to suggest that if you have been saved you will immediately lose all these obstacles to your happiness. I will tell you if you have been saved, you now have the Holy Spirit living inside you and you now have the tools needed to overcome these obstacles. I like to call these obstacles to happiness flesh darts because the devil will use these flesh darts to rob you of your joy in Christ if you let him. But you have the ability to overcome the devil and his attacks.

Finally, my brethren, be strong in the Lord, and in the power of his might. Put on the whole armour of God, that ye may be able to stand against the wiles of the devil. For we wrestle not against flesh and blood, but against principalities, against powers, against the rulers of the darkness of this world, against spiritual wickedness in high places. Wherefore take unto you the whole armour of God, that ye may be able to withstand in the evil day, and having done all, to stand. Stand therefore, having your loins girt about with truth, and having on the breastplate of righteousness; And your feet shod with the preparation of the gospel of peace; Above all, taking the shield of faith, wherewith ye shall be able to quench all the fiery darts of the wicked. And take the helmet of salvation, and the sword of the Spirit, which is the word of God: Praying always with all prayer and supplication in the Spirit, and watching thereunto with all perseverance and supplication for all saints.(Ephesians 6:10-18)

One of the tools you need to overcome these flesh darts is the Word of God as you have just seen in Ephesians 6:17. I am going to show you how to do this.

Fear, worry, doubt, anxiety, lack of faith, insecurity

Whosoever shall confess that Jesus is the Son of God, God dwelleth in him, and he in God. And we have known and believed the love that God hath to us. God is love; and he that dwelleth in love dwelleth in God, and God in him. Herein is our love made perfect, that we may have boldness in the day of judgment: because as he is, so are we in this world. There is no fear in love; but perfect love casteth out fear: because fear hath torment. He that feareth is not made perfect in love. We love him, because he first loved us. If a man say, I love God, and hateth his brother, he is a liar: for he that loveth not his brother whom he hath seen, how can he love God whom he hath not seen? (John 4:15–20)

Are not five sparrows sold for two farthings, and not one of them is forgotten before God? But even the very hairs of your head are all numbered. Fear not therefore: ye are of more value than many sparrows. Also I say unto you, Whosoever shall confess me before men, him shall the Son of man also confess before the angels of God. (Luke 12:6–8)

Be careful for nothing; but in everything by prayer and supplication with thanksgiving let your requests be made known unto God. And the peace of God, which passeth all understanding, shall keep your hearts and minds through Christ Jesus. (Philippians 4:6–7)

Indecisiveness, lack of direction, confusion, frustration, lack of guidance

Trust in the LORD with all thine heart; and lean not unto thine own understanding. In all thy ways acknowledge him, and he shall direct thy paths. (Proverbs 3:5–6)

And thine ears shall hear a word behind thee, saying, This is the way, walk ye in it, when ye turn to the right hand, and when ye turn to the left. (Isaiah 30:21)

For this God is our God for ever and ever: he will be our guide even unto death. (Psalm 48:14)

> And I will bring the blind by a way that they knew not; I will lead them in paths that they have not known: I will make darkness light before them, and crooked things straight. These things will I do unto them, and not forsake them. (Isaiah 42:16)

Helplessness, hopelessness, weakness, fear of failure, lack of accomplishment, physical limitations

> I can do all things through Christ which strengtheneth me. (Philippians 4:13)

> Ask, and it shall be given you; seek, and ye shall find; knock, and it shall be opened unto you: For every one that asketh receiveth; and he that seeketh findeth; and to him that knocketh it shall be opened. Or what man is there of you, whom if his son ask bread, will he give him a stone? Or if he ask a fish, will he give him a serpent? If ye then, being evil, know how to give good gifts unto your children, how much more shall your Father which is in heaven give good things to them that ask him? (Matthew 7:7–11)

Pride, self-righteousness, boastfulness, self-reliance, lack of humility

> For I say, through the grace given unto me, to every man that is among you, not to think of himself more highly than he ought to think; but to think soberly, according as God hath dealt to every man the measure of faith. (Romans 12:3)

Pride goeth before destruction, and an haughty spirit before a fall. Better it is to be of an humble spirit with the lowly, than to divide the spoil with the proud. (Proverbs 16:18-19)

And he said unto them, Ye are they which justify yourselves before men; but God knoweth your hearts: for that which is highly esteemed among men is abomination in the sight of God. (Luke 16:15)

Boast not thyself of tomorrow; for thou knowest not what a day may bring forth. Let another man praise thee, and not thine own mouth; a stranger, and not thine own lips. (Proverbs 27:1)

Unrighteous desires, temptations, lust, jealousy, envy

Wherefore let him that thinketh he standeth take heed lest he fall. There hath no temptation taken you but such as is common to man: but God is faithful, who will not suffer you to be tempted above that ye are able; but will with the temptation also make a way to escape, that ye may be able to bear it. (1Corinthians 10:12–13)

This I say then, Walk in the Spirit, and ye shall not fulfil the lust of the flesh. For the flesh lusteth against the Spirit, and the Spirit against the flesh: and these are contrary the one to the other: so that ye cannot do the things that ye would. But if ye be led of the Spirit, ye are not under the law. (Galatians 5:16–18)

> Dearly beloved, I beseech you as strangers and pilgrims, abstain from fleshly lusts, which war against the soul. (1Peter 2:11)

Guilt, shame, uncleanness, unworthiness, discouragement

> Knowing this, that our old man is crucified with him, that the body of sin might be destroyed, that henceforth we should not serve sin. For he that is dead is freed from sin. (Romans 6:6-7)

> Therefore if any man be in Christ, he is a new creature: old things are passed away; behold, all things are become new. And all things are of God, who hath reconciled us to himself by Jesus Christ, and hath given to us the ministry of reconciliation. To wit, that God was in Christ, reconciling the world unto himself, not imputing their trespasses unto them; and hath committed unto us the word of reconciliation. (2Corinthians 5:17-19)

> Likewise reckon ye also yourselves to be dead indeed unto sin, but alive unto God through Jesus Christ our Lord. (Romans 6:11)

If you have accepted Christ as your savior, you are equipped with all you need to defeat Satan. I have illustrated the use of one of the tools that Christians have in their arsenal (i.e., the Word of God) to fight the flesh darts of the devil and to restore happiness. The tools are truth, righteousness, the gospel of peace, faith, salvation, the Word of God and prayer.

CHAPTER 3

Misconceptions Concerning Happiness

Happiness can be provided by man alone. We don't need God.

We humans tend to trust the creature more than the creator. We trust the science of man more than the word of God. We trust the guidance and wisdom of man more than God's guidance. We try to convince ourselves that we are the masters of the universe, and we are in control of our own destinies. Humans believe they are their own gods. This is referred to as humanism. If you trust Darwin more than the word of God, then they have already begun to lead you off course. If you believe in evolution, where one species can evolve into another, then you have been misled. If you believe that we all came from amoebas out of the water, you are misguided. If you believe we came from monkeys, then they have led you astray. If you believe in the big bang theory and that the universe was created by accident, then you have been blinded by humanism. There is more science that proves that the word of God is true concerning creation and the beginning of humankind than there is to prove these humanistic theories. You can find all you need to know by searching for books that address scientific creationism. You don't hear about these materials out in the world because worldly humans and false science teachers don't want you to know the truth. Since God has been banned from our schools, especially in colleges, our young people are having their minds filled with humanistic theories every day.

> For the invisible things of him from the creation of the world are clearly seen, being understood by the things that are made, even his eternal power and Godhead; so that they are without excuse: Because that, when they knew God, they glorified him not as God, neither were thankful; but became vain in their imaginations, and their foolish heart was darkened. Professing themselves to be wise, they became fools, And changed the glory of the uncorruptible God into an image made like to corruptible man, and to birds, and four footed beasts, and creeping things. Wherefore God also gave them up to uncleanness through the lusts of their own hearts, to dishonour their own bodies between themselves: Who changed the truth of God into a lie, and worshipped and served the creature more than the Creator, who is blessed forever. Amen. For this cause God gave them up unto vile affections: for even their women did change the natural use into that which is against nature: And likewise also the men, leaving the natural use of the woman, burned in their lust one toward another; men with men working that which is unseemly, and receiving in themselves that recompence of their error which was meet. And even as they did not like to retain God in their knowledge, God gave them over to a reprobate mind, to do those things which are not convenient; Being filled with all unrighteousness, fornication, wickedness,

covetousness, maliciousness; full of envy, murder, debate, deceit, malignity; whisperers, Backbiters, haters of God, despiteful, proud, boasters, inventors of evil things, disobedient to parents, Without understanding, covenant breakers, without natural affection, implacable, unmerciful: Who knowing the judgment of God, that they which commit such things are worthy of death, not only do the same, but have pleasure in them that do them. (Romans 1:20–32)

O Timothy, keep that which is committed to thy trust, avoiding profane and vain babblings, and oppositions of science falsely so called. (1Timothy 6:20)

Happiness comes from material possessions.

People believe that if they were only wealthy, they would have everything they need to be happy. This is what the devil wants you to think. The fact is most that wealthy people, generally make up the larger number of the unhappiest people on earth. Money can't buy happiness, and it can't buy peace, love, joy, or contentment. Money can't remove sorrow or end death. Money can't bring you close to God. Jesus said it was easier for a camel to pass through the eye of a needle than for a rich man to enter into the kingdom of God.

Love not the world, neither the things that are in the world. If any man love the world, the love of the Father is not in him. For all that is in the world, the lust of the flesh, and the lust of the eyes, and the pride of life, is not of the Father, but is of the world. And the world passeth away, and the lust thereof:

but he that doeth the will of God abideth forever. (John 2:15–17)

He that trusteth in his riches shall fall; but the righteous shall flourish as a branch. (Proverbs 11:28)

Traitors, heady, highminded, lovers of pleasures more than lovers of God. (2Timothy 3:4)

Choosing rather to suffer affliction with the people of God, than to enjoy the pleasures of sin for a season. (Hebrews 11:25)

Lay not up for yourselves treasures upon earth, where moth and rust doth corrupt, and where thieves break through and steal: But lay up for yourselves treasures in heaven, where neither moth nor rust doth corrupt, and where thieves do not break through nor steal: For where your treasure is, there will your heart be also. (Matthew 6:19–21)

They that trust in their wealth, and boast themselves in the multitude of their riches; None of them can by any means redeem his brother, nor give to God a ransom for him. (Psalm 49:6–7)

And the disciples were astonished at his words. But Jesus answereth again, and saith unto them, Children, how hard is it for them that trust in riches to enter into the kingdom of God! It is easier for a camel to go through the eye of a needle, than for a rich man to enter into the kingdom of God. And they were astonished out of measure, saying among themselves, Who then can be saved? And Jesus looking upon them saith, With men it is impossible, but not with God: for with God all things are possible. Then Peter began to say unto him, Lo, we have left all, and have followed thee. And Jesus answered and said, Verily I say unto you, There is no man that hath left house, or brethren, or sisters, or father, or mother, or wife, or children, or lands, for my sake, and the gospel's, But he shall receive an hundredfold now in this time, houses, and brethren, and sisters, and mothers, and children, and lands, with persecutions; and in the world to come eternal life. But many that are first shall be last; and the last first. (Mark 10:24–31)

Happiness comes from relying only on myself.

Some people believe in being totally self-reliant. They believe they can't trust anyone except themselves. They have no faith or trust or belief in God. They believe they are completely in charge of their future. This type of belief structure only leads to disappointment and failure because we can't even rely on ourselves to be saved from eternal separation from God. It is God who provides salvation and only if we are willing to admit we need it. It is God who keeps us saved and we need to realize we don't have the ability to do that for ourselves either. We cannot provide our own salvation, our own joy, or own future. Without God man is lost.

> But we had the sentence of death in ourselves, that we should not trust in ourselves, but in God which raiseth the dead: Who delivered us from so great a death, and doth deliver: in whom we trust that he will yet deliver us. (2Corinthians 1:9–10)

Beware of dogs, beware of evil workers, beware of the concision. For we are the circumcision, which worship God in the spirit, and rejoice in Christ Jesus, and have no confidence in the flesh. (Philippians 3:2–3)

Thou art my King, O God: command deliverances for Jacob. Through thee will we push down our enemies: through thy name will we tread them under that rise up against us. For I will not trust in my bow, neither shall my sword save me. But thou hast saved us from our enemies, and hast put them to shame that hated us. In God we boast all the day long, and praise thy name for ever. Selah. (Psalm 44:4–8)

For by grace are ye saved through faith; and that not of yourselves: it is the gift of God: Not of works, lest any man should boast. For we are his workmanship, created in Christ Jesus unto good works, which God hath before ordained that we should walk in them. (Ephesians 2:8–10)

Happiness comes from success.

People somehow believe if they can only be successful in their family life or in their career or in their social outreach, this will bring them happiness. There is nothing wrong with being successful, but you should never count on your success bringing you happiness. I have been an aircraft mechanic all my life and I believe I have been rather successful at my career. I have traveled all over the world to provide my services. I have been called one of the best in the business. I have had thousands of satisfied customers and have earned the respect of those in the industry. I have even written a book on aircraft ownership. My career has provided me with everything that I have needed for many years. My wife says I am the hardest person to buy gifts for because I already have everything that I want. Nevertheless, all these things may bring temporary self-satisfaction and some self-worth but they do not provide eternal happiness from within which can only be achieved by trusting in God and obeying his will.

> Charge them that are rich in this world, that they be not high minded, nor trust in uncertain riches, but in the living God, who giveth us richly all things to enjoy; That they do good, that they be rich in good works, ready to distribute, willing to communicate; Laying up in store for themselves a good foundation against the time to come, that they may lay hold on eternal life. (1 Timothy 6:17–19)

> In the house of the righteous is much treasure: but in the revenues of the wicked is trouble. (Proverbs 15:6)

> By humility and the fear of the LORD are riches, and honour, and life. (Proverbs 22:4)

Success in life comes from following God's will for your life. Success gotten by ones self may bring temporary satisfaction, but success given to you by God for serving him brings happiness.

Happiness comes from spending time with my friends.

You can get joy from spending time with your brothers and sisters in Christ. You should separate yourselves from the unrighteous. I remember when I was a teenager, my oldest brother,

23

James, had gone out with some of his friends. Apparently, some of his friends were involved in illegal activities and my brother was with them when they were caught. My brother called my father and told him he was in jail and wanted my father to bail him out. He went on to explain that he had not done anything wrong but he was with some friends who had illegal paraphernalia and the police had taken him to jail too because he was with them. My father told him, "You got yourself in. Get yourself out." And he hung up. We were taught that if you hang out with bad people, even if you aren't like them, other people will think you are, and if you hang out with them long enough you will become like them. In the following verses, we are told not only to separate ourselves from unbelievers but also to separate from brothers in Christ if they are not doing God's will.

> It is better to trust in the LORD than to put confidence in princes. Trust ye not in a friend, put ye not confidence in a guide: keep the doors of thy mouth from her that lieth in thy bosom. (Psalm 118:8–9)

> For the son dishonoureth the father, the daughter riseth up against her mother, the daughter in law against her mother in law; a man's enemies are the men of his own house. Therefore I will look unto the LORD; I will wait for the God of my salvation: my God will hear me. (Micah 7:5–7)

> I wrote unto you in an epistle not to company with fornicators: Yet not altogether with the fornicators of this world, or with the covetous, or extortioners, or with idolaters; for then must ye needs go out of the world. But now I have written unto you not to

keep company, if any man that is called a brother be a fornicator, or covetous, or an idolater, or a railer, or a drunkard, or an extortioner; with such an one no not to eat. For what have I to do to judge them also that are without? Do not ye judge them that are within? But them that are without God judgeth. Therefore put away from among yourselves that wicked person. (1Corinthians 5:9–13)

Whosoever transgresseth, and abideth not in the doctrine of Christ, hath not God. He that abideth in the doctrine of Christ, he hath both the Father and the Son. If there come any unto you, and bring not this doctrine, receive him not into your house, neither bid him God speed: For he that biddeth him God speed is partaker of his evil deeds. (2John 1:9)

Happiness comes from all the things the world has to offer.

All the things the world has to offer come from the devil, and even though they may bring some temporary satisfaction to the flesh, the end is eternal damnation. The things the devil offers fall into three categories: the lust of the flesh, the lust of the eyes, and the pride of life. Jesus was tempted by all these things just as we are; only he remained without sin. Jesus defeated the devil's temptations by using the word of God to tell the devil to take everything he has to offer and go away. In order to accept the things of the world you must surrender to the devil and his will. For me that's not going to happen. You must decide if you're going to put your faith and trust in God or Satan. Many church schools today have been offered financial support from the government if they will follow the government's educational guidelines. Most of them have rejected this assistance because the government wants to take God out of education and these mandated guidelines compromise the truth.

> Love not the world, neither the things that are in the world. If any man love the world, the love of the Father is not in him. For all that is in the world, the lust of the flesh, and the lust of the eyes, and the pride of life, is not of the Father, but is of the world. And the world passeth away, and the lust thereof: but he that doeth the will of God abideth forever. (John 2:15–17)

> Then was Jesus led up of the spirit into the wilderness to be tempted of the devil. And when he had fasted forty days and forty nights, he was afterward an hungered. And when the tempter came to him, he said, If thou be the Son of God, command that these stones be made bread. But he answered and said, It is written, Man shall not live by bread alone, but by every word that proceedeth out of the mouth of God. Then the devil taketh him up into the holy city, and setteth him on a pinnacle of the temple, And saith unto him, If thou be the Son of God, cast thyself down: for it is written, He shall give his angels charge concerning thee: and in their hands they shall bear thee up, lest at any time thou dash thy foot against a stone. Jesus said unto him, It is written again, Thou shalt not tempt the Lord thy God. Again, the devil taketh him up into an exceeding high mountain, and sheweth him all the kingdoms of the world, and the glory of them; And saith unto him, All these things will I give thee, if

thou wilt fall down and worship me. Then saith Jesus unto him, Get thee hence, Satan: for it is written, Thou shalt worship the Lord thy God, and him only shalt thou serve. Then the devil leaveth him, and, behold, angels came and ministered unto him. (Matthew 4:1–11)

CHAPTER 4

Happiness Comes from Doing God's Will

I know what you are thinking: finding God's will is easier said than done. How do I know what God's will is? Well, the fact is you may not know completely what God's will is for your life, but there are a lot of things about God's will that we do know. We must start by doing the things we know while we wait for his direction and guidance concerning those things that have not yet been revealed. We as Christians often try to figure out what God wants us to do before it is time for us to do it. God is preparing you to do what he wants you to do, but if he hasn't told you what that is then you are not ready to hear it. Often God will wait for us to finish what he has already told us before he tells us anything else. Those who have been faithful in a little will be given much. It is like changing the oil in your car. If you try to put the new oil in before you drain the old oil, it won't fit. If you drain the oil before you put a pan under the drain you will make a mess. If you try to put the new oil in before you put the drain plug back in, then you have wasted time and resources and have not accomplished anything. Serving God is the same way: we need to finish what we already know we should be doing before He will tell us what is next.

Many years ago, when I was in an aircraft maintenance electrical class, I learned a valuable lesson. Before the instructor came into the classroom all the students had already come in and the instructor had laid out the study materials on the desk. Without exception, every student in the class had already started looking through the books and I believe all of us thought, *Oh my goodness, what have I gotten myself into?* Of course when you do this, you don't look at the front of the book; you look farther back so you can see what you are going to learn. The instructor finally came into the room, and he stood there watching all of us stare at the books in shock. Eventually, he said, "OK, guys, just set the books down and look up here for a minute." He obviously knew what we were all thinking.

He went on to say, "All things that seem to be complicated in life are just a whole bunch of simple things put together. If you start at the beginning of the book and just look at the first lesson, it only consists of memorizing a few simple symbols. When you are past the beginning steps, you will see how the rest is simple as well." If we will just trust God and follow the instructions he has already given us, then we will see how much more sense it makes when He tells us the rest.

We know it is God's will for us to be saved.

I'm not going to spend much time on this right now because we have already discussed the importance of being saved and how this is the beginning of the path to happiness. However, I would like for you to consider the following verses of scripture.

> And being brought on their way by the church, they passed through Phenice and Samaria, declaring the conversion of the Gentiles: and they caused great joy unto all the brethren. (Acts 15:3)

But if we walk in the light, as he is in the light, we have fellowship one with another, and the blood of Jesus Christ his Son cleanseth us from all sin. (John 1:7)

Happy art thou, O Israel: who is like unto thee, O people saved by the LORD, the shield of thy help, and who is the sword of thy excellency! and thine enemies shall be found liars unto thee; and thou shalt tread upon their high places. (Deuteronomy 33:29)

Happy is that people, that is in such a case: yea, happy is that people, whose God is the LORD. (Psalm 144:15)

Just realizing what God has done for me makes me want to shout for joy: the one and only almighty God has sacrificed his own son in order to save me. I want to share a story with you I heard years ago. There was a man who worked on a drawbridge. His job was to sit in the tower and wait for the ships to get close, and then he would sound the alarms, drop down the roadblocks, turn on the warning lights, and unlatch the drawbridge to be raised. In order that the road not be closed any longer than necessary, he would wait until the timing was just right and then raise the bridge. The timing had to be just right, though. The ships could not stop, so the bridge had to be all the way up before the ships entered the canal. One day this man decided to bring his young son to work with him. He wanted his son to see what his job was and thought the young boy would love the sights of the machines and equipment. He never thought there would be any danger because he thought he would keep his son in the tower and there was nothing that would hurt him there.

The morning went well. The man had shown his son all the equipment while there was nothing going on, and they both had a great time. The boy was fascinated with the large gears that were used to lift the bridge. Later in the day, there was a ship approaching, but it was still a long way off. The drawbridge man began to check the equipment in preparation for the ship's arrival. He checked the alarms and the lights, he checked the roadblock arms and the latches, and all appeared to be well. Now the ship was quickly approaching, and he sounded the alarms and released the latches. It was time to raise the bridge. At the last moment, he looked around to make sure his son was safe, only the boy wasn't there. While the man was preparing, the boy had snuck out to go look at the equipment again. The man knew he didn't have time to go look for the boy now. It was too late. He looked all around from the tower where he could see practically everything. At the last moment he saw his son climbing on the gears that would rotate when he raised the bridge. At this moment, the man had to decide if he was going to let all those thousands of people on the ship die and save his son or sacrifice his only son to save the people. This is the sacrifice God the Father made to save me.

> And it shall be said in that day, Lo, this is our God; we have waited for him, and he will save us: this is the LORD; we have waited for him, we will be glad and rejoice in his salvation. (Isaiah 25:9)

> Notwithstanding in this rejoice not, that the spirits are subject unto you; but rather rejoice, because your names are written in heaven. (Luke 10:20)

It is God's will that we put Him first in our lives.

Many people may not know or understand that this is the area where they are not doing God's will. Some will put their spouses over God. They may not be doing it intentionally, but actions speak louder than words. Your walk talks and your talk talks, but your walk talks louder than your talk talks. If the husband puts his desires for his wife above those commitments he has made to God, he has his priorities wrong. For example, if your wife has decided that God wants her to do volunteer work at your church or at a local shelter, but you don't want her to because she won't be there when you get home from work every day, then you are putting your desires ahead of God's will for her. A man is head over his wife, and she is told she should obey him, but if he asks her to do something he knows causes her to neglect what God wants her to do, then he is wrong. Ladies, if your husband's try to do what they feel like is God's will for their lives and you try to stop them from doing it, then you have your priorities wrong. The first commandment is to love the Lord thy God with all thy mind.

> Master, which is the great commandment in the law Jesus said unto him, Thou shalt love the Lord thy God with all thy heart, and with all thy soul, and with all thy mind. This is the first and great commandment. (Matthew 22:36–38)

It is God's will for men to love their wives even as Christ loved the church.

I think it should be mentioned that I have made this point next because there is a natural order of things according to God's word. God first, then your spouse, then your children, then everyone else, and last of all yourself. Many marriages have problems because men and women both try to place the needs of their children over their spouses. This is especially difficult if the children came from one of the two in the marriage but not the other. Even if your children are from a different marriage, you should always put your spouse ahead of the children. Marriage is for life; you should love each other as much as you love yourselves. Husbands and wives are intended to be together until death. If you put your children ahead of your spouse, it will be difficult for the marriage to last. I know this is especially difficult for mothers because of their motherly instinct to protect their children, but they need to trust their husbands and believe that if the husband tries to discipline their child, there is a reason. Your children will grow up and leave home and become their own persons. Your husband or wife will be with you till death.

> Wives, submit yourselves unto your own husbands, as unto the Lord. For the husband is the head of the wife, even as Christ is the head of the church: and he is the saviour of the body. Therefore as the church is subject unto Christ, so let the wives be to their own husbands in everything. Husbands, love your wives, even as Christ also loved the church, and gave himself for it; That he might sanctify and cleanse it with the washing of water by the word, That he might present it to himself a glorious church, not having spot, or wrinkle, or any such thing; but that it should be holy and without blemish. So ought men to love their wives as their own bodies. He that loveth his wife loveth himself. For no man ever yet hated his own flesh; but nourisheth and cherisheth it, even as the Lord the church: For we are members of his body, of his flesh, and of his bones. For this cause shall a man leave his father and mother, and shall be joined unto his wife, and they two shall be one flesh. (Ephesians 5:22–31)

> But I would have you know, that the head of every man is Christ; and the head of the woman is the man; and the head of Christ is God. Every man praying or prophesying, having his head covered,

dishonoureth his head. But every woman that prayeth or prophesieth with her head uncovered dishonoureth her head: for that is even all one as if she were shaven. For if the woman be not covered, let her also be shorn: but if it be a shame for a woman to be shorn or shaven, let her be covered. For a man indeed ought not to cover his head, forasmuch as he is the image and glory of God: but the woman is the glory of the man. For the man is not of the woman: but the woman of the man. Neither was the man created for the woman; but the woman for the man. For this cause ought the woman to have power on her head because of the angels. Nevertheless neither is the man without the woman, neither the woman without the man, in the Lord. For as the woman is of the man, even so is the man also by the woman; but all things of God. Judge in yourselves: is it comely that a woman pray unto God uncovered? Doth not even nature itself teach you, that, if a man have long hair, it is a shame unto him? But if a woman have long hair, it is a glory to her: for her hair is given her for a covering. (1Corinthians 11:3–15)

I probably shared more verses than I needed to here to make my point that a man should love his wife even as Christ loved the church and should follow God's will. But there are a few other things I'd like to mention here. The man should not only honor his wife and love her as much as he loves himself and even more so, but he should cherish her and nourish her. It is the man's responsibility to care for, protect, and provide for his wife. I also believe it is shameful for a woman to have a man's haircut or for a man to have long hair like a woman. As the apostle Paul says above, even nature itself teaches that women should have long hair. Somehow this symbolism is used to show that a wife should be in submission to her husband. I am not suggesting it is a sin for a woman to have short hair or for a man to have long hair, but according to the apostle, if that is the case, it will give other people a reason to wonder who is head over whom in that household. Long hair on a man and short hair on a woman are both symbolic of rebellion against God and his natural order. I am not trying to judge or condemn anyone here, but if you want to be happy, rebelling against God's way of doing things is not the best way to get there.

I have to be careful when I speak about the man being head over the wife. That doesn't mean the man should walk around beating his chest like an ape demanding that she obey his every command. If the husband loves the wife and cherishes her, then he will not ask her to do anything that is not godly or that is disrespectful or degrading. If the woman loves her husband like she should, she will take care of him out of love and he won't have to tell her to do anything. Men and women are different, and being different, each of them has a role to perform in their marriage. When they do this, they complement one another and become one complete person, "They two shall be one flesh" (Ephesians 5:31). The man is not complete without his wife and the wife is not complete without her husband.

We know that it is God's will for a man to work and provide for his household.

A man is responsible for taking care of himself and those of his household. This includes his daughters who have not married and his mother if she is a widow. The church is held accountable to care for those widows who have no surviving family. These widows are called *widows indeed*.

But if any provide not for his own, and specially for those of his own house, he hath denied the faith, and is worse than an infidel. (1Timothy 5:8)

For even when we were with you, this we commanded you, that if any would not work, neither should he eat. (2Thessalonians 3:10)

We know that it is God's will for both men and women to dress and act in a godly manner.

In like manner also, that women adorn themselves in modest apparel, with shamefacedness and sobriety; not with broided hair, or gold, or pearls, or costly array; But (which becometh women professing godliness) with good works. Let the woman learn in silence with all subjection. But I suffer not a woman to teach, nor to usurp authority over the man, but to be in silence. For Adam was first formed, then Eve. And Adam was not deceived, but the woman being deceived was in the transgression. Notwithstanding she shall be saved in childbearing, if they continue in faith and charity and holiness with sobriety. (1Timothy 2:9–15)

The word of God goes on to show us the perfect wife.

Who can find a virtuous woman? for her price is far above rubies. The heart of her husband doth safely trust in her, so that he shall have no need of spoil. She will do him good and not evil all the days of her life. She seeketh wool, and flax, and worketh willingly with her hands. She is like the merchants'ships; she bringeth her food from afar. She riseth also while it is yet night, and giveth meat to her household, and a portion to her maidens. She considereth a field, and buyeth it: with the fruit of her hands she planteth a vineyard. She girdeth her loins with strength, and strengtheneth her arms. She perceiveth that her merchandise is good: her candle goeth not out by night. She layeth her hands to the spindle, and her hands hold the distaff. She stretcheth out her hand to the poor; yea, she reacheth forth her hands to the needy. She is not afraid of the snow for her household: for all her household are clothed with scarlet. She maketh herself coverings of tapestry; her clothing is silk and purple. Her husband is known in the gates, when he sitteth among the elders of the land. She maketh fine linen, and selleth it; and delivereth girdles unto the merchant. Strength and honour are her clothing; and she shall rejoice in time to come. She openeth her mouth with wisdom; and in her tongue is the law of kindness. She looketh well to the ways of her household, and eateth not the bread of idleness. Her children arise up, and call her blessed; her husband also, and he praiseth her. Many daughters have done virtuously, but thou excellest them all. Favour is deceitful, and beauty is vain: but a woman that feareth the LORD, she shall be praised. Give her of the fruit of her hands; and let her own works praise her in the gates. (Proverbs 31:10–31)

Does this sound like a woman who is under a man's thumb to you? She comes and goes as she pleases. She buys and sells and does all the same things that her husband does. This is not a woman who is kept, as they say today, or a woman who is being controlled by anyone except God.

It is God's will that you bring up your children in the way of the Lord.

> And, ye fathers, provoke not your children to wrath: but bring them up in the nurture and admonition of the Lord. (Ephesians 6:4)

> Train up a child in the way he should go: and when he is old, he will not depart from it. (Proverbs 22:6)

> And if it seem evil unto you to serve the LORD, choose you this day whom ye will serve; whether the gods which your fathers served that were on the other side of the flood, or the gods of the Amorites, in whose land ye dwell: but as for me and my house, we will serve the LORD. (Joshua 24:15)

If you are doing everything you know that God wants you to do, then you are doing God's will right now. This doesn't mean God doesn't have more plans for you in the future. You know you should be serving God in some capacity. If you are doing that, then just keep doing it until He tells you what is next. God has given all his children gifts to be used in their service for Him. If He hasn't told you what that is yet, then the key to patience is doing something else while you wait for the answer. God wants you to know His will for your life more than you do, but He is waiting for the right timing. Trust me: if God doesn't think you're ready yet then you're not. There are many other things I could say concerning God's will for you, but they will be covered in other chapters of this book as we explore how God wants you to be happy.

And we beseech you, brethren, to know them which labour among you, and are over you in the Lord, and admonish you. (1Thessalonians 5:12)

And to esteem them very highly in love for their work's sake. And be at peace among yourselves. (1Thessalonians 5:13)

Now we exhort you, brethren, warn them that are unruly, comfort the feebleminded, support the weak, be patient toward all men. (1Thessalonians 5:14)

See that none render evil for evil unto any man; but ever follow that which is good, both among yourselves, and to all men. (1Thessalonians 5:15)

Rejoice evermore. (1Thessalonians 5:16)

Pray without ceasing. (1Thessalonians 5:17)

In every thing give thanks: for this is the will of God in Christ Jesus concerning you. (1Thessalonians 5:18)

Quench not the Spirit. (1Thessalonians 5:19)

Despise not prophesyings. (1 Thessalonians 5:20)

Prove all things; hold fast that which is good. (1 Thessalonians 5:21)

Abstain from all appearance of evil. (1 Thessalonians 5:22)

And the very God of peace sanctify you wholly; and I pray God your whole spirit and soul and body be preserved blameless unto the coming of our Lord Jesus Christ. (1 Thessalonians 5:23)

These verses summarize God's immediate will for you:

1. Be aware of those around you who labor in God's work on your behalf and show them proper respect These would be the leaders in your church: pastors, deacons, teachers, and others. (1 Thessalonians 5:12–13a)
2. Be at peace among yourselves. There should be no strife between the brothers and sisters in Christ. (1 Thessalonians 5:13b)
3. Warn those who are unruly, those who claim to be brothers and sisters but don't live like they are. (1 Thessalonians 5:14a)
4. Comfort those who are mentally not able to take care of themselves. (1 Thessalonians 5:14b)
5. Support the weak, give to those who need the help. (1 Thessalonians 5:14c)
6. Be patient toward all men, forgive, and don't hold grudges. Be understanding when other people do things differently than you do. Just because people do things differently than you do doesn't make them wrong. (1 Thessalonians 5:14d)
7. If someone does you evil then pay them back by doing good to them whether they are saved or lost. (1 Thessalonians 5:15)
8. Always be happy, rejoicing, and in a good mood. (1 Thessalonians 5:16)
9. Pray continuously, all day every day, keeping the channel of communication between you and God open all the time. (1 Thessalonians 5:17)

10. Thank God for everything that happens in your life whether it seems to be good or bad at the time because it is God's will for you. (1 Thessalonians 5:18)

11. Quench not the spirit. When we do things that are contrary to God's word it shuts down the Holy Spirit that lives inside of you. Grieve not the Spirit. (1 Thessalonians 5:19)

12. Despise not prophesyings. Prophesying can mean foretelling or forth-telling. In our time it would be preaching or forth-telling. Don't get mad at the preacher because he said something that convicted you. (1 Thessalonians 5:20)

13. Prove all things. This means everything should be tested by the word of God. If it doesn't agree with what the word teaches it is not from God. (1 Thessalonians 5:21a)

14. Hold fast to the good. To follow God's will, always do good or always do the right thing. (1 Thessalonians 5:21b)

15. Abstain from all appearance of evil. If the lost see you do something that is questionable they will judge you and God for it. If an immature brother or sister sees you do something they think is wrong it will cause them to have doubts. Even though many things are permissible to the mature Christian, it is not a good idea to do those things where others who cannot do the same things with a clear conscience can see them. This is not being hypocritical; this is being thoughtful and considerate to others as not to offend them. (1 Thessalonians 5:22)

16. If you will do these things you will be sanctified, (i.e., separated for God's use) and kept by the power of God while waiting for the coming of our Lord. (1 Thessalonians 5:23)

Are you ready for God to show you what is next? Are you currently doing all these things? If you are, then you have been separated for God's use and soon you will know what that is. If you're not, then don't expect any other guidance until you do.

CHAPTER 5

Happiness Comes from Trusting God

This is the "Don't worry, be happy" verse:

> Be careful for nothing; but in everything by prayer and supplication with thanksgiving let your requests be made known unto God. And the peace of God, which passeth all understanding, shall keep your hearts and minds through Christ Jesus. (Philippians 4:6–7)

Let me paraphrase so you will see what I mean. Don't worry about anything; trust God to provide all your needs by asking him for what you need, and you can have the confidence to be thankful for his answer before you even get it. If you will trust God this much, he will give you a peace that people will not understand. You must put your trust in God alone; this is the only way you will find happiness.

> Happy is he that hath the God of Jacob for his help, whose hope is in the LORD his God: Which made heaven, and earth, the sea, and all that therein is: which keepeth truth for ever: Which executeth

judgment for the oppressed: which giveth food to the hungry. The LORD looseth the prisoners: The LORD openeth the eyes of the blind: the LORD raiseth them that are bowed down: the LORD loveth the righteous: The LORD preserveth the strangers; he relieveth the fatherless and widow: but the way of the wicked he turneth upside down. The LORD shall reign forever, even thy God, O Zion, unto all generations. Praise ye the LORD. (Psalm 146:5–10)

He that handleth a matter wisely shall find good: and whoso trusteth in the LORD, happy is he. (Proverbs 16:20)

Come unto me, all ye that labour and are heavy laden, and I will give you rest. Take my yoke upon you, and learn of me; for I am meek and lowly in heart: and ye shall find rest unto your souls. For my yoke is easy, and my burden is light. (Matthew 11:28–30)

And there ye shall eat before the LORD your God, and ye shall rejoice in all that ye put your hand unto, ye and your households, wherein the LORD thy God hath blessed thee. Ye shall not do after all the things that we do here this day, every man whatsoever is right in his own eyes. For ye are not as yet come to the rest and to the inheritance, which the LORD your God giveth you. (Deuteronomy 12:7–9)

Reasons God gives us to rejoice

Rejoice in how God has blessed us.

> Seven days shalt thou keep a solemn feast unto the LORD thy God in the place which the LORD shall choose: because the LORD thy God shall bless thee in all thine increase, and in all the works of thine hands, therefore thou shalt surely rejoice. (Deuteronomy 16:15)

Rejoice because there is none greater than God.

> And Hannah prayed, and said, My heart rejoiceth in the LORD, mine horn is exalted in the LORD: my mouth is enlarged over mine enemies; because I rejoice in thy salvation. There is none holy as the LORD: for there is none beside thee: neither is there any rock like our God. (1Samuel 2:1–2)

Rejoice because of God's wondrous works.

> Then on that day David delivered first this psalm to thank the LORD into the hand of Asaph and his brethren. Give thanks unto the LORD, call upon his name, make known his deeds among the people. Sing unto him, sing psalms unto him, talk ye of all his wondrous works. Glory ye in his holy name: let the heart of them rejoice that seek the LORD. Seek the LORD and his strength, seek his face continually. Remember his marvellous works that he hath done, his wonders, and the judgments of his mouth. (1Chronicles 16:7–12)

Rejoice in our salvation.

> And they that know thy name will put their trust
> in thee: for thou, LORD, hast not forsaken them
> that seek thee. Sing praises to the LORD, which
> dwelleth in Zion: declare among the people his
> doings. (Psalm 9:10–11)

> But I have trusted in thy mercy; my heart shall
> rejoice in thy salvation. I will sing unto the LORD,
> because he hath dealt bountifully with me. (Psalm
> 13:5–6)

> The fool hath said in his heart, There is no God.
> They are corrupt, they have done abominable works,
> there is none that doeth good. (Psalm 14:1)

Rejoice because of God's mercy.

> Hear, O LORD, and have mercy upon me: LORD,
> be thou my helper. Thou hast turned for me my
> mourning into dancing: thou hast put off my
> sackcloth, and girded me with gladness; To the end
> that my glory may sing praise to thee, and not be
> silent. O LORD my God, I will give thanks unto
> thee forever. The righteous shall rejoice when God
> takes revenge on their enemies. (Psalm 30:10–12)

> The righteous shall rejoice when he seeth the
> vengeance: he shall wash his feet in the blood of
> the wicked. So that a man shall say, Verily there is
> a reward for the righteous: verily he is a God that
> judgeth in the earth. (Psalm 58:10–11)

Rejoice when we sing praises unto God for His protection.

> Thou shalt increase my greatness, and comfort me on every side. I will also praise thee with the psaltery, even thy truth, O my God: unto thee will I sing with the harp, O thou Holy One of Israel. My lips shall greatly rejoice when I sing unto thee; and my soul, which thou hast redeemed. My tongue also shall talk of thy righteousness all the day long: for they are confounded, for they are brought unto shame, that seek my hurt. (Psalm 71:21–24)

Rejoice and be glad for God's holiness.

> For thou, LORD, art high above all the earth: thou art exalted far above all gods. Ye that love the LORD, hate evil: he preserveth the souls of his saints; he delivereth them out of the hand of the wicked. Light is sown for the righteous, and gladness for the upright in heart. Rejoice in the LORD, ye righteous; and give thanks at the remembrance of his holiness. (Psalm 97:9–12)

Rejoice at God's deliverance of the poor.

> Yet setteth he the poor on high from affliction, and maketh him families like a flock. The righteous shall see it, and rejoice: and all iniquity shall stop her mouth. Whoso is wise, and will observe these things, even they shall understand the loving kindness of the LORD. (Psalm 107:41–43)

Rejoice over the day that Jesus became the cornerstone of salvation.

> I will praise thee: for thou hast heard me, and art
> become my salvation. The stone which the builders
> refused is become the head stone of the corner. This
> is the LORD's doing; it is marvellous in our eyes.
> This is the day which the LORD hath made; we will
> rejoice and be glad in it. (Psalm 118:21–24)

Rejoice because we have the Bible.

> Thy word is true from the beginning: and every
> one of thy righteous judgments endureth forever.
> Princes have persecuted me without a cause: but
> my heart standeth in awe of thy word. I rejoice at
> thy word, as one that findeth great spoil. I hate and
> abhor lying: but thy law do I love. Seven times a day
> do I praise thee because of thy righteous judgments.
> Great peace have they which love thy law: and
> nothing shall offend them. LORD, I have hoped
> for thy salvation, and done thy commandments.
> (Psalm 119:160–166)

Rejoice with the wife that God has given you.

> Let thy fountain be blessed: and rejoice with the
> wife of thy youth. Let her be as the loving hind and
> pleasant roe; let her breasts satisfy thee at all times;
> and be thou ravished always with her love. (Proverbs
> 5:18–19)

Many people have hang-ups about sex. Sex is not a dirty word
when it is shared between a husband and his wife. It is not just
intended for procreation of the species. It is also intended to be a
pleasurable experience between a man and his wife. Many years
ago, the first book I ever wrote was called *God's Marriage and Man's*

Divorce. Marriage was God's idea because from the start He knew it was not good for man to be alone. Woman was therefore created to be man's helper, company, and companion. This relationship is very important in God's plan for man. When I wrote this book I didn't have the financial resources I have today, and I was unable to get it published. However, because there is so much confusion and misunderstanding concerning this relationship between a man and his wife, I am seriously considering revisiting this topic in future writings if I am tasked by the Holy Spirit to do so.

> Marriage is honourable in all, and the bed undefiled: but whoremongers and adulterers God will judge. (Hebrews 13:4)

Rejoice when you raise your children to fear God.

> Withhold not correction from the child: for if thou beatest him with the rod, he shall not die. Thou shalt beat him with the rod, and shalt deliver his soul from hell. My son, if thine heart be wise, my heart shall rejoice, even mine. Yea, my reins shall rejoice, when thy lips speak right things. Let not thine heart envy sinners: but be thou in the fear of the LORD all the day long. For surely there is an end; and thine expectation shall not be cut off. Hear thou, my son, and be wise, and guide thine heart in the way. Be not among winebibbers; among riotous eaters of flesh: For the drunkard and the glutton shall come to poverty: and drowsiness shall clothe a man with rags. Hearken unto thy father that begat thee, and despise not thy mother when she is old. Buy the truth, and sell it not; also wisdom, and instruction, and understanding. The father of the righteous shall greatly rejoice: and he that begetteth

a wise child shall have joy of him. Thy father and thy mother shall be glad, and she that bare thee shall rejoice. My son, give me thine heart, and let thine eyes observe my ways. For a whore is a deep ditch; and a strange woman is a narrow pit. She also lieth in wait as for a prey, and increaseth the transgressors among men. Who hath woe? who hath sorrow? who hath contentions? who hath babbling? who hath wounds without cause? who hath redness of eyes? They that tarry long at the wine; they that go to seek mixed wine. Look not thou upon the wine when it is red, when it giveth his colour in the cup, when it moveth itself aright. At the last it biteth like a serpent, and stingeth like an adder. Thine eyes shall behold strange women, and thine heart shall utter perverse things. (Proverbs 23:13–33)

Rejoice together with those who sow and those who reap lost souls.

Say not ye, There are yet four months, and then cometh harvest? behold, I say unto you, Lift up your eyes, and look on the fields; for they are white already to harvest. And he that reapeth receiveth wages, and gathereth fruit unto life eternal: that both he that soweth and he that reapeth may rejoice together. And herein is that saying true, One soweth, and another reapeth. I sent you to reap that whereon ye bestowed no labour: other men laboured, and ye are entered into their labours. And many of the Samaritans of that city believed on him for the saying of the woman, which testified, He told me all that ever I did. So when the Samaritans were come unto him, they besought him that he would tarry with them: and he abode there two days. And many more believed because of his own word. (John 4:35–41)

Rejoice in the hope and glory of God.

Therefore being justified by faith, we have peace with God through our Lord Jesus Christ: By whom also we have access by faith into this grace wherein we stand, and rejoice in hope of the glory of God. (Romans 5:1–2)

Rejoice when your brothers and sisters in Christ are honored or receive great rewards.

That there should be no schism in the body; but that the members should have the same care one for another. And whether one member suffer, all the members suffer with it; or one member be honoured, all the members rejoice with it. Now ye are the body of Christ, and members in particular. (1Corinthians 12:25–27)

Rejoice that you can have confidence in your brethren in Christ.

I rejoice therefore that I have confidence in you in all things. (2Corinthians 7:16)

Rejoice that at the coming of Christ our labor will not be in vain.

Holding forth the word of life; that I may rejoice in the day of Christ, that I have not run in vain, neither laboured in vain. Yea, and if I be offered upon the sacrifice and service of your faith, I joy,

and rejoice with you all. For the same cause also do
ye joy, and rejoice with me. (Philippians 2:16–18)

Rejoice when you suffer for the church (i.e., the body of Christ).

Who now rejoice in my sufferings for you, and fill
up that which is behind of the afflictions of Christ
in my flesh for his body's sake, which is the church:
Whereof I am made a minister, according to the
dispensation of God which is given to me for you,
to fulfil the word of God. (Colossians 1:24–25)

Rejoice in the Lord always.
Rejoice in the Lord alway: and again I say, Rejoice. (Philippians 4:4)
Rejoice evermore. (1Thessalonians 5:16)
Rejoice that ye are kept by the power of God.

Blessed be the God and Father of our Lord Jesus
Christ, which according to his abundant mercy
hath begotten us again unto a lively hope by the
resurrection of Jesus Christ from the dead, To
an inheritance incorruptible, and undefiled, and
that fadeth not away, reserved in heaven for you,
Who are kept by the power of God through faith
unto salvation ready to be revealed in the last time.
Wherein ye greatly rejoice, though now for a season,
if need be, ye are in heaviness through manifold
temptations: That the trial of your faith, being
much more precious than of gold that perisheth,
though it be tried with fire, might be found unto
praise and honour and glory at the appearing of
Jesus Christ. (1Peter 1:3–7)

Rejoice that the rich shall be made low and the low shall be exalted.

> Let the brother of low degree rejoice in that he is exalted: But the rich, in that he is made low: because as the flower of the grass he shall pass away. (James 1:9–10)

With all this rejoicing going on, how is anyone supposed to be unhappy around here? It is obvious that God doesn't want His children to have long faces. What kind of testimony do we have for Christ if the world sees us being sad all the time? When people are sad, other people feel sorry for them. They certainly don't try to find what the sad people have. God expects people to look at Christians and feel like they need to get whatever it is we have. What do people in the world feel when they look at the expression on your face? If it is sad, then you need to get your happy back on. If it is your circumstances, then you need to be able to rise above the circumstances and rejoice in what God has done for you. If you dwell on the bad, the bad is all that will show on your face. If someone has done you wrong, then forgive and forget. If you have done someone else wrong, then ask them and God to forgive you and move on. If you are harboring a secret sin in your life, if you have done something you are ashamed of and don't want to admit it, if you feel guilt and don't know what to do about it, this will rob you of your happy. You need to take care of this. When I hire a new employee, I explain to that person that I understand that everyone makes mistakes. This I expect, but since we work on aircraft, it is essential that mistakes be corrected and corrected properly. Therefore, no one will get in trouble for making a mistake; however, if they make a mistake and try to hide it or cover it up somehow, they will be fired. You know the difference between a mechanic and a technician? They both make mistakes, but technicians know how to fix them. I think this is how God feels when we mess up. He knows we are going to mess up; that is expected, but we need to realize we can't hide our mistakes from God. We need to admit our mistake and confess it to God and ask Him for His forgiveness. The truth shall set you free. In this case we are the mechanics and God is the technician, but He only has to fix what we mess up.

CHAPTER 6

Happiness Comes from Surrender to the Holy Spirit

I'm sure you have heard it said that happiness comes from within. It is not something you can get from your surroundings or from other people. In the beginning we saw the things that make people unhappy; these are all works of the flesh, things the devil can use against us to steal our happy. This isn't how God wants his children to live. I told you there was a war between the flesh and the spirit that goes on inside a Christian continually. If we commit sins, it grieves the Spirit of God that dwells inside us and that results in unhappiness. The flip side of that same coin is to do things that are pleasing to the Spirit of God and that will result in happiness. Yes, happiness is a by-product of righteousness. Simply stated, happiness is a result of doing right. It is not enough to try to stop living for the flesh; we must start living for or submitting to the Spirit. Submitting to the Spirit results in good works, or righteousness, or the fruits of the Spirit showing in our lives. One of these fruits is joy or happiness.

> And that ye put on the new man, which after God is
> created in righteousness and true holiness. Wherefore
> putting away lying, speak every man truth with his
> neighbour: for we are members one of another. Be

ye angry, and sin not: let not the sun go down upon your wrath: Neither give place to the devil. Let him that stole steal no more: but rather let him labour, working with his hands the thing which is good, that he may have to give to him that needeth. Let no corrupt communication proceed out of your mouth, but that which is good to the use of edifying, that it may minister grace unto the hearers. And grieve not the holy Spirit of God, whereby ye are sealed unto the day of redemption. Let all bitterness, and wrath, and anger, and clamour, and evil speaking, be put away from you, with all malice: And be ye kind one to another, tenderhearted, forgiving one another, even as God for Christ's sake hath forgiven you. (Ephesians 4:24–32)

Be ye therefore followers of God, as dear children; And walk in love, as Christ also hath loved us, and hath given himself for us an offering and a sacrifice to God for a sweet smelling savour. But fornication, and all uncleanness, or covetousness, let it not be once named among you, as becometh saints; Neither filthiness, nor foolish talking, nor jesting, which are not convenient: but rather giving of thanks. For this ye know, that no whoremonger, nor unclean person, nor covetous man, who is an idolater, hath any inheritance in the kingdom of Christ and of God. Let no man deceive you with vain words: for because of these things cometh the wrath of God upon the children of disobedience. Be not ye therefore partakers with them. For ye were sometimes darkness, but now are ye light in the Lord: walk as children of light: (For the fruit of the Spirit is in all goodness and righteousness and truth;) Proving what is acceptable unto the Lord. And have no fellowship with the unfruitful works of darkness, but rather reprove them. For it is a shame even to speak of those things which are done of them in secret. (Ephesians 5:1–12)

If the fruits of the Spirit are not shining out in your life, you are either not a child of God or you have not surrendered to the Holy Spirit. When a person is possessed by the devil, the devil controls that person. When a person is indwelt by the Holy Spirit, even though he can no longer be demon possessed, the Holy Spirit will only control as much of that person as the person allows him to. The following verses give a list of the fruits of the Spirit.

But the fruit of the Spirit is love, joy, peace, longsuffering, gentleness, goodness, faith, Meekness, temperance: against such there is no law. And they that are Christ's have crucified the flesh with the affections and lusts. If we live in the Spirit, let us also walk in the Spirit. (Galatians 5:22–25)

Happy is the man who fears the Lord and follows His commandments. Again happiness is the by-product of righteousness.

And ye became followers of us, and of the Lord, having received the word in much affliction, with joy of the Holy Ghost. (1 Thessalonians 1:6)

Blessed is every one that feareth the LORD; that walketh in his ways. For thou shalt eat the labour of thine hands: happy shalt thou be, and it shall be well with thee. Thy wife shall be as a fruitful vine by the sides of thine house: thy children like olive plants round about thy table. Behold, that thus shall the man be blessed that feareth the LORD. (Psalm 128:1)

Positive Thinking

Even though I don't like to call it positive thinking, I am going to use this term because it is one that most people are familiar with. In a way, I guess you could say happiness is a frame of mind, an attitude. This attitude (renewing of the mind), is one of the things you should change as a Christian, and the result is a disposition of happiness. I don't like to use the term positive thinking because this seems to leave God and the Holy Spirit out of the picture. I believe any person can improve his or her life by having a positive attitude but only Christians can have a renewal of the mind by the power of the Holy Spirit.

> That ye put off concerning the former conversation the old man, which is corrupt according to the deceitful lusts; And be renewed in the spirit of your mind. (Ephesians 4:22–23)

If you renew your mind, change your attitude, and think positive thoughts, this will result in internal happiness that people can't help but see. We are instructed to change the way we think. We should concentrate on things that are above.

> Lay not up for yourselves treasures upon earth, where moth and rust doth corrupt, and where thieves break through and steal: But lay up for yourselves treasures in heaven, where neither moth nor rust doth corrupt, and where thieves do not break through nor steal: For where your treasure is, there will your heart be also. (Matthew 6:19–21)

And the peace of God, which passeth all understanding, shall keep your hearts and minds through Christ Jesus. Finally, brethren, whatsoever things are true, whatsoever things are honest, whatsoever things are just, whatsoever things are pure, whatsoever things are lovely, whatsoever things are of good report; if there be any virtue, and if there be any praise, think on these things. Those things, which ye have both learned, and received, and heard, and seen in me, do: and the God of peace shall be with you. (Philippians 4:7–9)

If ye then be risen with Christ, seek those things which are above, where Christ sitteth on the right hand of God. Set your affection on things above, not on things on the earth. For ye are dead, and your life is hid with Christ in God. (Colossians 3:1–3)

Another result of being submitted to the Holy Spirit is sanctification.

Sanctification simply means to be set apart for God's purposes. God cannot use a dirty vessel; therefore, in order for him to use you, you must be made holy. The word *holy* also means sanctified. This is another term for you submitting all of yourself to the control of the Spirit of God. The Lord says, "ye shall be Holy; for I am Holy" (Leviticus 11:44).

Furthermore then we beseech you, brethren, and exhort you by the Lord Jesus, that as ye have received of us how ye ought to walk and to please God, so ye would abound more and more. For ye know what commandments we gave you by the Lord Jesus. For this is the will of God, even your sanctification, that ye should abstain from fornication: That every one of you should know how to possess his vessel in sanctification and honour; Not in the lust of concupiscence, even as the Gentiles which know not God: That no man go beyond and defraud his brother in any matter: because that the Lord is the avenger of all such, as we also have forewarned you and testified. For God hath not called us unto uncleanness, but unto holiness. (1 Thessalonians 4:1–7)

That I should be the minister of Jesus Christ to the Gentiles, ministering the gospel of God, that the offering up of the Gentiles might be acceptable, being sanctified by the Holy Ghost. (Romans 15:16)

Wherefore gird up the loins of your mind, be sober, and hope to the end for the grace that is to be brought unto you at the revelation of Jesus Christ; As obedient children, not fashioning yourselves according to the former lusts in your ignorance: But as he which hath called you is holy, so be ye holy in all manner of conversation; Because it is written, Be ye holy; for I am holy. God, that the offering up of the Gentiles might be acceptable, being sanctified by the Holy Ghost. (1 Peter 1:13–16)

Remember these things are part of the submission to the Holy Spirit, but the more you submit the happier you will be.

Another result of submitting to the Holy Spirit is contentment.

If you can learn to trust God and accept the fact that no matter what happens to you it is according to God's will for your life, then you can learn to be content, or in other words, to have a positive attitude no matter what the circumstances are.

> But godliness with contentment is great gain. For we brought nothing into this world, and it is certain we can carry nothing out. And having food and raiment let us be therewith content. But they that will be rich fall into temptation and a snare, and into many foolish and hurtful lusts, which drown men in destruction and perdition. For the love of money is the root of all evil: which while some coveted after, they have erred from the faith, and pierced themselves through with many sorrows. But thou, O man of God, flee these things; and follow after righteousness, godliness, faith, love, patience, meekness. (1 Timothy 6:6–11)
>
> In everything give thanks: for this is the will of God in Christ Jesus concerning you. (1 Thessalonians 5:18)

When you have submitted to the Holy Spirit enough that you can always have an attitude of thankfulness no matter what is going on in your life, then you will have found your happy. The rain will fall on the good and evil alike (Matthew 5:45). The difference between that rain causing happiness or unhappiness depends on whether or not you accept the rain as something God thinks you need. Most people have heard of the coat of many colors. This is the story about Joseph, one of God's chosen vessels in the Old Testament. Joseph was one of the descendants of Abraham. Joseph was his father Jacob's favorite son, and Jacob gave him a coat of many colors. Joseph's brothers were so jealous of him they threw him into a pit and left him to die. A band of merchants came by and pulled him out of the pit and made him a slave. He was sold to the Egyptians as a slave and was eventually thrown into prison in Egypt. Obviously, this does not sound like someone who has found favor with God, but we don't know what God's plan is. God used Joseph to save the nation of Israel by giving him the gift of interpreting the Pharaoh's dream. Joseph proclaims at the end that his brothers meant it for evil but God allowed all these things to happen to him in order to put him in a position to save Israel. Sometimes the world will do things to Christians they mean for evil but God allows it to happen because he plans to use it for good in the end. When you can be thankful to God when things are going bad for you, then you are close to finding your happy.

> But I say unto you, Love your enemies, bless them that curse you, do good to them that hate you, and pray for them which despitefully use you, and persecute you; That ye may be the children of your Father which is in heaven: for he maketh his sun to rise on the evil and on the good, and sendeth rain on the just and on the unjust. For if ye love them which love you, what reward have ye? do not even the publicans the same? And if ye salute your brethren only, what do ye more than others? Do not even the publicans so? Be ye therefore perfect, even as your Father which is in heaven is perfect. (Matthew 5:44–48)

And we know that all things work together for good
to them that love God, to them who are the called
according to his purpose. (Romans 8:28)

So now let me give you an example of positive thinking. I am
going to use the Lord's Prayer as what I like to call a "happy quick
start."

"Our Father": This reminds me I am a chosen child
of God entitled to his inheritance.

"Which art in heaven": There is a mansion in heaven
reserved just for me.

"Hallowed be thy name": Praise and worship the
Lord for all he has done for me.

"Thy Kingdom come": This is not my final home
and I have a reservation in his kingdom.

"Thy will be done": If I can always be thankful for
what God is doing, I'll always be happy.

"On earth as in heaven": The devil is in control of
this world right now, but his days are numbered.

"Give us this day": This is a day that the Lord has
made; let us rejoice and be glad in it.

"Our daily bread": Thank you, Lord, for your daily
provision for me and my household.

"And forgive us our trespasses": Thank you, Lord, for the blood of the Lamb that cleansed me.

"As we forgive those who have trespassed against us": Forgive and you shall be forgiven.

"Lead us not into temptation": Thank you, Lord, for providing a way to escape temptation.

"But deliver us from evil": Thank you for the victory we have over the devil, death, hell, sin, and the grave.

CHAPTER 7

Happiness Comes from Close Fellowship with God

The closer we are to God, the happier we will become. God does not choose favorites, so anyone can get as close as they want. God is our Father and as a father he wants to be close to his children, but you can only be close to your father if you live according to his rules. Our Father in heaven has a lot of rules, but keeping them should not be grievous to his children because we love him and want to make him happy. Keep in mind I am talking about fellowship with God here, not relationship. Once you are saved your relationship is secured, but that doesn't mean you will always get along with your father.

> That which was from the beginning, which we have heard, which we have seen with our eyes, which we have looked upon, and our hands have handled, of the Word of life; (For the life was manifested, and we have seen it, and bear witness, and shew unto you that eternal life, which was with the Father, and was manifested unto us;) That which we have seen and heard declare we unto you, that ye also may have fellowship with us: and truly our fellowship is with the Father, and with his Son Jesus Christ. And

these things write we unto you, that your joy may be full. (John 1:1–4)

If there be therefore any consolation in Christ, if any comfort of love, if any fellowship of the Spirit, if any bowels and mercies, Fulfil ye my joy, that ye be likeminded, having the same love, being of one accord, of one mind. Let nothing be done through strife or vainglory; but in lowliness of mind let each esteem other better than themselves. Look not every man on his own things, but every man also on the things of others. Let this mind be in you, which was also in Christ Jesus: (Philippians 2:1–5)

Ye adulterers and adulteresses, know ye not that the friendship of the world is enmity with God? whosoever therefore will be a friend of the world is the enemy of God. Do ye think that the scripture saith in vain, The spirit that dwelleth in us lusteth to envy? But he giveth more grace. Wherefore he saith, God resisteth the proud, but giveth grace unto the humble. Submit yourselves therefore to God. Resist the devil, and he will flee from you. Draw nigh to God, and he will draw nigh to you. Cleanse your hands, ye sinners; and purify your hearts, ye double minded. (James 4:4–8)

How does one draw closer to God? I'm glad you asked. Some of the things that result in being closer to God we have already discussed: submission to the Holy Spirit, trust in God, sanctification, and a renewing of the mind. I am going to give you some others.

We draw closer to God by doing things that are pleasing to God.

Thou art worthy, O Lord, to receive glory and honour and all power: for thou hast created all things, and for thy pleasure they are and were created. (Revelation 4:11)

I will say to the north, Give up; and to the south, Keep not back: bring my sons from far, and my daughters from the ends of the earth; Even every one that is called by my name: for I have created him for my glory, I have formed him; yea, I have made him. (Isaiah 43:6–7)

Giving thanks unto the Father, which hath made us meet to be partakers of the inheritance of the saints in light: Who hath delivered us from the power of darkness, and hath translated us into the kingdom of his dear Son: In whom we have redemption through his blood, even the forgiveness of sins: Who is the image of the invisible God, the firstborn of every creature: For by him were all things created, that are in heaven, and that are in earth, visible and invisible, whether they be thrones, or dominions, or principalities, or powers: all things were created by him, and for him: And he is before all things, and by him all things consist. And he is the head of the body, the church: who is the beginning, the firstborn from the dead; that in all things he might have the preeminence. For it pleased the Father that in him should all fullness dwell. (Colossians 1:12–19)

We draw closer to God by increasing our faith.

> To open their eyes, and to turn them from darkness
> to light, and from the power of Satan unto God, that
> they may receive forgiveness of sins, and inheritance
> among them which are sanctified by faith that is in
> me. (Acts 26:18)

> For therein is the righteousness of God revealed
> from faith to faith: as it is written, The just shall live
> by faith. (Romans 1:17)

> So then faith cometh by hearing, and hearing by the
> word of God. (Romans 10:17)

Jesus said if we only had faith as a grain of a mustard seed we
could tell a mountain move from here and go over there and it would
do it. I don't think I have seen anyone with that much faith. We
could apparently all use some improvement in that area. The point
is that it pleases God very much when we have faith in what He can
do if we ask and believe. (Matthew 17:20).

We draw closer to God by reading and studying the Bible.

> Consider how I love thy precepts: quicken me,
> O LORD, according to thy loving kindness. Thy
> word is true from the beginning: and every one of
> thy righteous judgments endureth forever. Princes
> have persecuted me without a cause: but my heart
> standeth in awe of thy word. I rejoice at thy word, as
> one that findeth great spoil. I hate and abhor lying:
> but thy law do I love. (Psalm 119:159–163)

For the word of God is quick, and powerful, and sharper than any two edged sword, piercing even to the dividing asunder of soul and spirit, and of the joints and marrow, and is a discerner of the thoughts and intents of the heart. (Hebrews 4:12)

Mine eyes prevent the night watches, that I might meditate in thy word. (Psalm 119:148)

But his delight is in the law of the LORD; and in his law doth he meditate day and night. (Psalm 1:2)

For the commandment is a lamp; and the law is light; and reproofs of instruction are the way of life. (Proverbs 6:23)

Thy word is a lamp unto my feet, and a light unto my path. (Psalms 119:105)

I cannot overemphasize the importance of learning God's word and putting as much of it as you can to memory. This is how God communicates with us. The Holy Spirit will use God's word to tell you what to do in your daily life and to tell you what to do in God's service. We know how to talk to God from reading God's word. We learn what God expects from us, how to ask for things, and what we shouldn't ask for. Without the word of God in your heart the Holy Spirit has few ways to communicate with the believer.

Jesus answered and said unto him, If a man love me, he will keep my words: and my Father will love him, and we will come unto him, and make our abode with him. He that loveth me not keepeth not my sayings: and the word which ye hear is not mine, but the Father's which sent me. These things have

I spoken unto you, being yet present with you. But
the Comforter, which is the Holy Ghost, whom the
Father will send in my name, he shall teach you all
things, and bring all things to your remembrance,
whatsoever I have said unto you. Peace I leave
with you, my peace I give unto you: not as the
world giveth, give I unto you. Let not your heart be
troubled, neither let it be afraid. (John 14:23–27)

B-asic I-nstructions B-efore L-eaving E-arth

We draw closer to God by praying.

Possibly the most important thing that we need to do to have
close fellowship with God is pray. The word is primarily how God
speaks to us; prayer is how we speak to God. God knows what you
want and what you have need of before you even ask, but He wants
you to ask. Prayer is not just for asking for things either. Prayer is for
thanking God for all He does for us each day. Prayer is worshipping
and praising God for His glory. Prayer is for getting closer to God.
I think of it this way: God is not some far away, off in the distance
almighty untouchable entity who doesn't think about me at all. If I
thought of God that way, I would be scared to say anything. The fact
is I am one with Jesus the son of God through the indwelling of the
Holy Spirit and therefore God, Jesus' father is the same as God my
father. I talk to him just like I did my earthly father.

Be careful for nothing; but in everything by prayer
and supplication with thanksgiving let your requests
be made known unto God. (Philippians 4:6)

Be glad in the LORD, and rejoice, ye righteous: and shout for joy, all ye that are upright in heart. (Psalm 32:11)

Rejoice in the LORD, O ye righteous: for praise is comely for the upright. Praise the LORD with harp: sing unto him with the psaltery and an instrument of ten strings. Sing unto him a new song; play skillfully with a loud noise. For the word of the LORD is right; and all his works are done in truth. He loveth righteousness and judgment: the earth is full of the goodness of the LORD. By the word of the LORD were the heavens made; and all the host of them by the breath of his mouth. (Psalm 33:1–6)

Pray without ceasing. In everything give thanks: for this is the will of God in Christ Jesus concerning you. Quench not the Spirit. (1 Thessalonians 5:18–19)

Jesus told us not to recite prayers in vain repetitions (Matthew 6:7).This means don't just memorize the words to pre-packaged prayers and repeat them over and over from memory. This kind of prayer means nothing to God. He expects you to talk to Him just like you would talk to your physical father. When I talk to Him, I tell Him about my day, areas where I did what I think He wanted me to and areas where I still need further guidance. I thank Him for the good things that happened in that day. I ask Him for help in areas where things didn't go so well. I know that He already knows all of this, but I also know that He wants me to talk to Him like a friend. I should also point out that in the verse above it says to pray without ceasing. This is done by keeping the channel of communication open between you and God 24/7. God talks to me all day long, especially when I need on-the-spot guidance. This is why I told you to memorize the word of God. I also talk to Him all day long. I don't have to wait for him to answer my call. Prayer is absolutely essential in having a close relationship with God, and a close relationship with God is essential to happiness in a Christian's life.

> And this is the confidence that we have in him, that, if we ask any thing according to his will, he heareth us: And if we know that he hear us, whatsoever we ask, we know that we have the petitions that we desired of him. (John 5:14–15)

> And whatsoever ye shall ask in my name, that will I do, that the Father may be glorified in the Son. If ye shall ask any thing in my name, I will do it. If ye love me, keep my commandments. (John 14:13–15)

> And in that day ye shall ask me nothing. Verily, verily, I say unto you, Whatsoever ye shall ask the Father in my name, he will give it you. Hitherto have ye asked nothing in my name: ask, and ye shall receive, that your joy may be full. (John 16:23–24)

> Is any among you afflicted? let him pray. Is any merry? let him sing psalms. Is any sick among you? let him call for the elders of the church; and let them pray over him, anointing him with oil in the name of the Lord: And the prayer of faith shall save the sick, and the Lord shall raise him up; and if he have committed sins, they shall be forgiven him. Confess your faults one to another, and pray one for another, that ye may be healed. The effectual fervent prayer of a righteous man availeth much. (James 5:13–16)

I suppose a hundred books could be written on the topic of

prayer. That is not my purpose here, but there is one verse that I would like to point out that emphasizes both the importance of prayer and the importance of your relationship with your wife or your husband.

> Likewise, ye husbands, dwell with them according to knowledge, giving honour unto the wife, as unto the weaker vessel, and as being heirs together of the grace of life; that your prayers be not hindered. (1 Peter 3:7)

First, dwell with them according to knowledge. In my opinion, this refers to the fact that men and women are not the same. As a husband I cannot expect my wife to react to things the same way that I do. Generally speaking, women are more emotional and sensitive than men are. Treating her with honor means being careful what you say to her. I can't even tell you how many times I have offended my wife accidentally. I would be playing around, but she took it seriously, and years later I still hear about it. One time I told her she should train herself the way I was trained in Bible College. I was told a preacher should have a rhino hide. That simply means you need to learn to let stuff roll off your back like water rolls off a rhino. People are going to say things that offend you, especially as a preacher or a preacher's wife. You must learn to not be offended. Don't kid yourself: women are just not made that way; they will be offended by things you say and things others say, so you need to think before you speak. The second thing is the woman is the weaker vessel. I believe this refers to the fact that God made women to be men's helpers and therefore, generally speaking, they are better followers than men are. They are weaker emotionally and physically than men are, making them more susceptible to suggestion and sometimes temptation. I believe God made them this way because as men we would never be able to get a woman to listen to anything we said if He didn't.

This is not an attack on women. I believe it is a compliment because men are blind in certain areas and their wives can definitely be helpful to their husbands when it comes to seeing certain things. For example, if your wife tells you a certain woman has eyes for you, even if you never noticed the person she is talking about, you had better listen to her. Women have a sixth sense concerning certain things that men are clueless about. "Being heirs together of the grace of life" reminds us that husbands and wives are one and therefore are on this journey through life and to heaven together. Whatever one does affects the other, so you should never make any major decisions without including one another. The couple that prays together, stays together. It also points out the fact that God gave the gift of the ability to create life to husbands and wives. Finally, the last thing I want to point out in this verse is if you don't maintain your relationship with your wife or husband as you should, it will hinder your prayers. If you are fighting with your wife every day or asking her to do things that are contrary to God's will for her life or mistreating her, physically or emotionally, this is why God is not listening to your prayers. This is why you don't get answers from God. This is why you have lost your close fellowship with God and your happiness.

I would like to conclude this topic with a look at the beatitudes: Matthew 5:3 through 5:11.The Greek word that is translated to *blessed* here is *Makarios* (Mak-ar'-ee-os). The word can be translated to mean extremely blessed or happy. I want you to substitute happy where the Bible says blessed because happy is what we are looking for in this lesson.

> Blessed (happy) are the poor in spirit: for theirs is the kingdom of heaven.

> Blessed (happy) are they that mourn: for they shall be comforted.

Blessed (happy) are the meek: for they shall inherit the earth.

Blessed (happy) are they which do hunger and thirst after righteousness: for they shall be filled.

Blessed (happy) are the merciful: for they shall obtain mercy.

Blessed (happy) are the pure in heart: for they shall see God.

Blessed (happy) are the peacemakers: for they shall be called the children of God.

Blessed (happy) are they which are persecuted for righteousness' sake: for theirs is the kingdom of heaven.

Blessed (happy) are ye, when men shall revile you, and persecute you, and shall say all manner of evil against you falsely, for my sake.

Rejoice, and be exceeding glad: for great is your reward in heaven: for so persecuted they the prophets which were before you.

Ye are the salt of the earth: but if the salt have lost his savour, wherewith shall it be salted? it is thenceforth good for nothing, but to be cast out, and to be trodden under foot of men.

Ye are the light of the world. A city that is set on an hill cannot be hid. Neither do men light a candle, and put it under a bushel, but on a candlestick; and it giveth light unto all that are in the house. Let your light so shine before men, that they may see your good works, and glorify your Father which is in heaven.(Matthew 5:3–16)

Jesus is talking to people who have accepted him as their savior. The first portion of each of these statements refers to their current condition here on earth. They were the poor, those who mourned with sorrow, the humble, those who wanted to do right, those who showed mercy, those who had pure hearts, those who strived to make peace, and those persecuted for doing right. The people who display these types of attitudes have already given their hearts to God. They already make sacrifices for the sake of Jesus Christ. Jesus says those of you in this condition should rejoice and be exceedingly glad because you have such a great reward waiting for you when you get to heaven. He goes on to say you are the people who bring light into a dark world and you should not hide your light. Christians should proclaim what God has done for them to the entire world. When people see your good works they will recognize what God has done for you and God will get the glory.

Are you salt that has lost its savor? Are you a light hid under a bushel? If you are a Christian and you are not sharing the gospel of Christ with the world in one way or another, then this is why you are not rejoicing and exceedingly glad. You don't have to be a preacher to share the gospel. You do it by the way you live and by the way you treat others. Let your light shine, and be ready to give an answer to those who would ask about the reason you are different. Have you lost the excitement you had when you got saved? Is God not a big deal anymore? If you will work on restoring your fellowship with God, He will respond by restoring your happy.

CHAPTER 8

Happiness Comes from Helping Others

I try to help other people as often as I can. I do help other people every time the Holy Spirit tells me to. Most are very grateful and surprised at the offerings. Just a few days ago I went to the local diner for breakfast at six in the morning with one of my coworkers. I went straight to the dining room, got a cup of coffee, and headed for my seat. As I turned from the coffee pot, I saw two older gentlemen sitting at one of the tables next to the wall on the far side of the room. I have seen these two fellows many times before. The one is a loud, rambunctious sort who gives the impression he believes he rules the world. The other is a rather quiet gentleman who generally only speaks when spoken to and is soft-spoken at that. When I saw them, the Holy Spirit immediately told me I needed to give them $100 apiece. I never felt these two gentlemen needed my help but when God tells me to do something, I do it. Most of the time, it brings me great joy. I must admit that normally when people tell me how grateful they are I usually tell them I am the one who should be grateful to them. This is because it makes me feel good to help others. It makes the Spirit inside me jump for joy. I pulled $200 out of my wallet, walked over to the table and, with a $100 bill in each hand, I reached out toward each of them. I looked at them both and said, "I'm not sure what the need is, but God just told me to give each of you gentlemen $100" and I turned, walked away, and sat down.

The loud one immediately stood, came over, and started telling me how thankful he was and how much it meant to him because he really needed it. He wanted a hug and seemed to be overwhelmed with joy. The other gentleman sat there staring at the $100 bill the whole time this was going on.

After the first one was finished, the second man looked at me and said, "Why did you do this?"

I said, "Because God told me to, and I always do what God says." Then I asked him, "Are you telling me you don't need it?"

He said, "No, I always need help. I just never get it and I'm just wondering why you would do this when I have never said I needed anything."

I repeated once more, "I am doing it because God told me to. Use it however God tells you to." I have had many people tell me they don't give money out like that because they don't know who they should give it to. They are afraid that whoever they give it to will probably spend it on drugs are alcohol. My response to that is, I don't know who to give it to either, and I only do it when God tells me to. Second, it is not my responsibility what they do with it after they have it; that is between them and God. I do believe that out of all the things I do as a Christian, the one thing that brings the most joy to me is helping others. I work in order to be able to help those in need.

> Let him that stole steal no more: but rather let him labour, working with his hands the thing which is good, that he may have to give to him that needeth. (Ephesians 4:28)

> He that despiseth his neighbor sinneth: but he that hath mercy on the poor, happy is he. (Proverbs 14:21)

> I have shewed you all things, how that so labouring
> ye ought to support the weak, and to remember
> the words of the Lord Jesus, how he said, It is more
> blessed to give than to receive. (Acts 20:35)

Before my wife and I were married I told her I needed to discuss something with her that was very important to me. I told her there were only a couple of things that would not be acceptable if we were married. The first would be unfaithfulness and the second would be her not allowing me to help others. When I said the second condition, she actually laughed a little. I asked her what was funny, and she said she intended to tell me the same thing.

> Be not forgetful to entertain strangers: for thereby
> some have entertained angels unawares. (Hebrews
> 13:2)

> If a brother or sister be naked, and destitute of daily
> food, And one of you say unto them, Depart in
> peace, be ye warmed and filled; notwithstanding ye
> give them not those things which are needful to the
> body; what doth it profit? (James 2:15–16)

> But whoso hath this world's good, and seeth his
> brother have need, and shutteth up his bowels of
> compassion from him, how dwelleth the love of
> God in him? (John 3:17)

About a month ago my wife was at a secondhand store and an older lady was in line in front of her at the checkout counter. The older lady was purchasing a large item for her house that would not fit in her car. Sometimes the Lord puts us in the right place at the right time. My wife, seeing the lady's predicament, asked her if she wanted her to haul this item to her house since my wife was driving a pickup truck. The lady was very grateful and even offered to pay for the couple of items my wife was planning to purchase. My wife tried to refuse the payment, but the woman insisted. Sometimes it is okay to accept payment because those people need to be blessed as well. You don't want to rob them of a blessing either. As they drove to the lady's house, they got into a discussion about the damage from the hurricane the previous year. My wife told the lady I could fix her house for her because the contractors were trying to rob her and she couldn't afford it. The lady said she would try to pay me something, and my wife told her, "Good luck with that." Before you ask, I don't mind when my wife helps others and I don't mind when she volunteers me to help either. I always appreciate the opportunity to help when I can. Unfortunately, these days I'm not physically able to do what I used to do, and I don't have all the resources I once had. I'm not complaining. God has been extremely good to me, but no-one stays young or lives forever. I'm just trying to find new and different ways to help people now.

> Distributing to the necessity of saints; given to hospitality. (Romans 12:13)

> For I was an hungered, and ye gave me meat: I was thirsty, and ye gave me drink: I was a stranger, and ye took me in: Naked, and ye clothed me: I was sick, and ye visited me: I was in prison, and ye came unto me. Then shall the righteous answer him, saying, Lord, when saw we thee an hungered, and fed thee? or thirsty, and gave thee drink? When saw we thee a stranger, and took thee in? or naked, and clothed thee? Or when saw we thee sick, or in prison, and came unto thee? And the King shall answer and say unto them, Verily I say unto you, Inasmuch as ye have done it unto one of the least

of these my brethren, ye have done it unto me. (Matthew 25:35–40)

A while back, I had gone to work early and was watching the news in the airport lounge and drinking coffee when I glanced outside through the glass front door. I saw something lying on the sidewalk by the door. I opened the door, and there was a young woman curled up and asleep on the sidewalk. I woke her up and asked her if she needed anything. She said she was thirsty, so I took her into the airport terminal building and got her something to drink. She sat down and began to watch the news on the television. It was obvious she was homeless because it looked like she had been wearing the same dirty clothes for a long time. Her hair was ragged, and I could tell she hadn't been well nourished. As she sat there watching the news, I thought about how I could help her. There was a political story on the news, and we ended up getting into a rather aggressive discussion over politics. She wanted to blame her situation on a political party, and I did not agree. One day I will write a book called *Religion and Politics,* but that is for another day. This discussion went on for about half an hour, and it was getting time for me to get to work. I told her I couldn't leave her sitting in the airport building without anyone else there and that she would have to leave. As she headed for the door, I stopped her and handed her a $100 bill. She looked at me like I was crazy.

She said, "You and I are nothing alike. We don't agree on anything. We have been arguing about politics for thirty minutes. Why on earth would you give me money?"

I told her there were two reasons: one, because God told me to, and second, whether we agree on anything or not is less important than the obvious fact you need the money more than I do.

Here is what I'm trying to tell you. A person doesn't have to be saved to need your help. A person doesn't need to be clean and bathed to need your help. You don't have to agree with someone for them to need your help. Jesus was criticized for keeping company with the poor and with sinners and with the homeless. His reply to this accusation was that the healthy don't need a physician. The rich don't need a handout; the saved don't need salvation. It is more important to let your light shine to the lost world than to help those who don't need it. If you have lost your happy, find someone who is poor and help that person. Find someone who is hungry, and buy him or her a meal. Find someone who is homeless, and get that person to a shelter. Find someone who needs work on their car or house, and give him or her a hand. If you do this, God will bless you and you will find your happy.

> And if ye lend to them of whom ye hope to receive, what thank have ye? for sinners also lend to sinners, to receive as much again. But love ye your enemies, and do good, and lend, hoping for nothing again; and your reward shall be great, and ye shall be the children of the Highest: for he is kind unto the unthankful and to the evil. Be ye therefore merciful, as your Father also is merciful. Judge not, and ye shall not be judged: condemn not, and ye shall not be condemned: forgive, and ye shall be forgiven: Give, and it shall be given unto you; good measure, pressed down, and shaken together, and running over, shall men give into your bosom. For with the same measure that ye mete withal it shall be measured to you again. (Luke 6:34–38)

I own a couple of rental properties in Orange, Texas, and there was a young couple living in one of the apartments. The man was a young guy, but he was ill and feeble and unable to work. The woman was trying to take care of him and their little girl and keep a job at a fast-food restaurant. They were having trouble paying the bills every month and I was trying to help. One day I went over to the apartment to work on something, and she was telling me about her difficulties. She said the thing she regretted most was that her daughter's birthday was coming soon and she could not afford to get her anything. I didn't say anything to the young woman, but as soon as I left, I called some friends and began to make arrangements for a birthday party like you've never seen. A couple of days before the birthday, I called the mother and told her she needed to bring her husband and her baby to my house at two in the afternoon. I think the little girl was two years old, but she had a wonderful birthday party with balloons, cake, party games, music, and boat rides. Everyone had a good time, and then they all went home. Regardless of what happened after that, it was a good thing to do.

Later, they stopped paying their rent altogether and eventually moved out of the apartment still owing about four months rent. They left the apartment a giant mess for us to clean up. It took a long time and some significant finances to clean up the mess, which included making trips to the dump, paying for an exterminator, replacing bad appliances, and so on, but it is OK. I would do the same thing for them again if God told me to. I learned a long time ago if you are going to help someone, it is going to cost you something. You know the saying: if it doesn't cost anything, it isn't worth anything. Don't help anyone expecting something in return. Don't lend expecting repayment. Do it because God told you to, and your reward will be worth more than what you spent. You still want your happy back?

There was this little girl around five years-old. I guess she was in her daycare one morning. Her teacher wanted to give all the kids something to keep them occupied for a short time while she got things ready for the day. When she got to this little girl, she gave her a puzzle with a picture of the globe on it and moved on to the next person. After the teacher had finished handing all the children something to do out of her bag of toys, she walked back to the front of the class and sat down. When she looked out across the room, she noticed this one girl was sitting there quietly staring up at her. She asked the girl what she needed, and the girl told her she was finished and didn't have anything to do. The teacher asked her if she had missed her while handing out toys and she replied she got something, but was already finished with it. The teacher went over and looked at the puzzle laying on the girl's desk. It was a puzzle of the globe and it looked rather complicated for a small child.

She asked the girl, "But sweetie, how did you get this done so fast?"

The little girl told her, "When I turned it over there was a picture of Jesus on the other side. I figured if I put Jesus back where he belonged, then the world be right too."Out of the mouths of babes and sucklings Thou hast perfected praise" (Matthew 21:16). If you have lost your fervency and enthusiasm about Jesus, you need to put Jesus back where he belongs in your life and then you will find your happy.

CHAPTER 9

Happiness Comes from an Attitude of Gratitude

I have found that with that positive attitude adjustment comes an attitude of thankfulness. I have also found that if we spend all of our time thinking about the wonderful things God has done for us and how thankful we are, there is little time to think about what makes us unhappy. You know what they say: "An idle mind is the devil's workshop." When you get up in the morning thank God you are still alive. When you have breakfast thank God you have food. When you kiss your wife goodbye thank God He gave her to you. When you see your children thank God He gave them to you; you know children are a gift from God. When you go to bed at night thank God you have a roof over your head and a bed to sleep in. Thank God you have a vehicle to drive. Thank God for your country you live in. Thank God for your church and your preacher. Thank God for your job.

Now here is where it gets a little unusual for you. When you have a fender bender, thank God it wasn't a more serious wreck. When one of your children has an injury, thank God it wasn't more serious. When you see other people with infirmities, thank God that you don't have what they do. Thank God for making you who you are. Thank God for being a small person or a large person. Thank

God for making you male or female. By the way, God doesn't make mistakes. If you aren't happy with your gender, that is your mistake, not God's. That didn't cost you anything; I threw it in for free. Thank God for your personality. Thank God for your family—yes, even the ones you don't get along with. If you believe everything happens for a reason and all things work together for good for them that love God, you should be able to thank God for all that happens to you everyday whether it seems good or bad at the time. This is an attitude of gratitude. If you have this attitude, you will always be happy.

> Offer unto God thanksgiving; and pay thy vows unto the most High. (Psalm 50:14)

> O come, let us sing unto the LORD: let us make a joyful noise to the rock of our salvation. (Psalm 95:1)

> Let us come before his presence with thanksgiving, and make a joyful noise unto him with psalms. (Psalm 95:2)

> Enter into his gates with thanksgiving, and into his courts with praise: be thankful unto him, and bless his name. (Psalm 100:4)

I mentioned before that you should pray without ceasing, that is, keep the channel of communication open all the time. Try this; it works for me—most of the time. When something happens suddenly at work that didn't exactly go your way, the flesh would normally cry out cursing. Keep in mind that God is on the line with you, so you have a hot mic, so to speak. (If you're a pilot you understand that.) God is listening to everything you say, so your reaction is going to be from the Spirit inside you rather than the flesh. Don't you think it is a good idea to speak to God in the Spirit and not the flesh? You will cry out something like "Praise the Lord" or maybe "Thank you, Jesus" because at least it wasn't worse. I realize if you are not used to responding this way it may take some time for it to become a habit and, even then, you are still human and will slip from time to time.

I have mentioned previously that you should have enough confidence in God to be thankful for the answers to your prayers before you even finish the prayer. I should probably tell you that the eventual answer to the prayer may not be the answer you expected or wanted, but it will be what is best for you even if you don't think so. I don't know about you, but when I was growing up, I didn't always get what I asked for from my father, but he always tried to get what was best for me. You should not be disappointed at God's answer to your prayer no matter what it is because he knows what is best for you better than you do. You mothers out there are disappointed when God doesn't answer your prayers the way you would like, but when your child or grandchild asks you for candy at the store, do they always get it? If they don't, then you are being upset with God for being the same with you as you are with your children or grandchildren. Now do you understand? As hard as it may be, we need to realize God is doing what is best for us; his ways are higher than our ways and his thoughts higher than our thoughts. Like the song says, "Sometimes I thank God for unanswered prayers." Wow, I got so excited back there I almost called Grandma a hypocrite. Glad I controlled myself.

> Be careful for nothing; but in everything by prayer and supplication with thanksgiving let your requests be made known unto God. (Philippians 4:6)

> Continue in prayer, and watch in the same with thanksgiving. (Colossians 4:2)

> Seek ye the LORD while he may be found, call ye upon him while he is near: Let the wicked forsake his way, and the unrighteous man his thoughts: and let him return unto the LORD, and he will have mercy upon him; and to our God, for he will abundantly pardon. For my thoughts are not your thoughts, neither are your ways my ways, saith the LORD. For as the heavens are higher than the earth, so are my ways higher than your ways, and my thoughts than your thoughts. (Isaiah 55:6–9)

When I pray with my family it seems like I spend the majority of the time thanking God for what he has done for us. It is difficult to be sad, discouraged, unhappy, disappointed, depressed, angry, or discouraged when you are being thankful. It is like some kind of miracle or something. I don't know, I can't explain it, but I know this is how it works. If you spend a lot of time thinking about all that God has done for you and thanking him for it, you will not have time to be unhappy.

> Being enriched in everything to all bountifulness, which causeth through us thanksgiving to God. For the administration of this service not only supplieth the want of the saints, but is abundant also by many thanksgivings unto God. (2Corinthians 9:11–12)

> Saying, Amen: Blessing, and glory, and wisdom, and thanksgiving, and honour, and power, and might, be unto our God for ever and ever. Amen. (Revelation 7:12)

> Now thanks be unto God, which always causeth us to triumph in Christ, and maketh manifest

the savour of his knowledge by us in every place. (2Corinthians 2:14)

Did you know that in the Old Testament there were a lot of animals that could not be eaten by God's people because they were considered to be unclean? I am sure most of you are aware of this. But do you know why, or better yet, how it is that they are not considered unclean anymore, or at least not for Christians? The answer is that they are sanctified (i.e., set apart for God's purposes) by the word of God and prayer through the thanksgiving of the believers in Christ. In other words, Christians are given permission from God to eat any kind of meat they want as long as they thank God for it in prayer.

> Now the Spirit speaketh expressly, that in the latter times some shall depart from the faith, giving heed to seducing spirits, and doctrines of devils; Speaking lies in hypocrisy; having their conscience seared with a hot iron; Forbidding to marry, and commanding to abstain from meats, which God hath created to be received with thanksgiving of them which believe and know the truth. For every creature of God is good, and nothing to be refused, if it be received with thanks giving: For it is sanctified by the word of God and prayer. (1Timothy 4:1–5)

Thanksgiving is a big part of prayer and praise and even sanctification. Thanksgiving is also essential to happiness. I believe we should celebrate Thanksgiving every day. Some may have more material blessings than others but material things in this life are not what we should be most thankful for. All that is in this life will pass away and what will be left are the things we have accomplished for eternity: helping others, saving lost souls, spreading God's word, enjoying times of joy and fellowship with other believers. You will carry good works with you to heaven and you will be rewarded according to your works. If you will set your heart and mind on things above and live your life accordingly then you will be storing up rewards in heaven and you have much to be happy about. These things are what we should be thankful for. I'm thankful for the life that God has given me and the knowledge he has given me to put emphasis on the things that will last for eternity.

> I thank thee, and praise thee, O thou God of my fathers, who hast given me wisdom and might, and hast made known unto me now what we desired of thee for thou hast now made known unto us the king's matter. (Daniel 2:23)

CHAPTER 10

Happiness Comes from Seeing the Fruits of Our Labor

The things we do that last for eternity should be the things that matter the most to Christians. This is what Jesus called laying up treasures in heaven. Time and time again in the Bible, the apostle Paul talks about how happy it makes him that his converts are being faithful to God and continue to serve Him.

> For what is our hope, or joy, or crown of rejoicing? Are not even ye in the presence of our Lord Jesus Christ at his coming? For ye are our glory and joy. (1 Thessalonians 2:19–20)

> And brought them out, and said, Sirs, what must I do to be saved? And they said, Believe on the Lord Jesus Christ, and thou shalt be saved, and thy house. And they spake unto him the word of the Lord, and to all that were in his house. And he took them the same hour of the night, and washed their stripes; and was baptized, he and all his, straightway. And when he had brought them into his house, he set meat before them, and rejoiced, believing in God with all his house. (Acts 16:30–34)

> I thank my God upon every remembrance of you,
> Always in every prayer of mine for you all making
> request with joy, For your fellowship in the gospel
> from the first day until now; Being confident of this
> very thing, that he which hath begun a good work
> in you will perform it until the day of Jesus Christ.
> (Philippians 1:3–6)

Joy can be found in serving other Christians as they do God's work. The great commission to spread the gospel to all the world is for every Christian to take part in. Not all are preachers or teachers but we all have a role in this important work.

> For we have great joy and consolation in thy love,
> because the bowels of the saints are refreshed by
> thee, brother. (Philemon 1:7)

> For so hath the Lord commanded us, saying, I have
> set thee to be a light of the Gentiles, that thou
> shouldest be for salvation unto the ends of the earth.
> And when the Gentiles heard this, they were glad,
> and glorified the word of the Lord: and as many as
> were ordained to eternal life believed. And the word
> of the Lord was published throughout all the region.
> But the Jews stirred up the devout and honourable
> women, and the chief men of the city, and raised
> persecution against Paul and Barnabas, and expelled
> them out of their coasts. But they shook off the dust
> of their feet against them, and came unto Iconium.
> And the disciples were filled with joy, and with the
> Holy Ghost. (Acts 13:47–52)

The things we have covered are by no means the only reasons we have to be happy but it is a good place to start. Now I would like to summarize the things we have talked about, leave you some quick references to read in your Bible, and share with you a few other things we haven't talked about.

Joy comes from trusting God. (Psalms 146:5, Proverbs 28:25, 1 Timothy 6:20–21, Proverbs 16:20)

Joy comes from faith. (Hebrews 11:1, Acts 26:18, Romans 1:17, Romans 10:17, Ephesians 2:8–9, James 1:5–6)

Joy comes from helping others. (Proverbs 14:21, John 13:16–17, Luke 14:13–14, Luke 6:38)

Joy comes from fearing God. (Proverbs 28:14, Psalm 128:1–4)

Joy comes from a righteous lifestyle. (1 Thessalonians 1:6, 1 Thessalonians 5:12–22, Psalm 84:11, Proverbs 13:21, Matthew 6:33)

Joy comes from having a clear conscience. (Romans 14:22–23, Proverbs 17:22, Hebrews 13:5, 1 Timothy 6:6, Luke 3:14)

Joy comes with persecution for Christ's name sake. (1 Peter 4:12–14, 1 Peter 3:13–15)

Joy comes from heavenly thoughts. (Matthew 5:11–12, Philippians 4:8)

Joy comes from prayer. (Philippians 4:6–7, Matthew 21:22, 1 John 5:14–15, James 5:16)

Joy comes from being a child of God. (Psalm 144:15, 1 John 1:7)

Joy comes from God's correction or guidance. (Job 5:17, Psalm 37:23, Luke 1:79)

Joy comes from doing God's will. (2 Thessalonians 2:13–14, John 15:3)

Joy comes from fellowship with God. (1 John 1:1–4, Philippians 2:1-2, James 4:8)

Joy comes from sanctification. (1 Thessalonians 4:2–4, 2 Thessalonians 3:6)

Joy comes from seeing the fruits of our labor. (1 Thessalonians 2:19–20)

Joy comes from overcoming temptation. (James 1:1–6, Hebrews 4:15–16)

Joy comes from being able to accept everything as God's will. (1 Timothy 6:6–10, Philippians 4:11, Hebrews 13:5)

Joy comes from God's word. (Hebrews 4:12, Revelation 1:3, Psalm 119:130, 2Peter 1:19, John 5:39, 2 Timothy 3:15–16)

Joy comes from victory over death, hell, and the grave. (James 4:7,1 Corinthians 15:51–58, 1 Thessalonians 4:14–18)

Joy comes from keeping God's Laws. (John 15:11, John 13:14–17, John 15:9–17)

Joy comes from fellowship with other Christians. (Romans 15:32, Hebrews 10:24–25)

Now for a few personal observations.

I want to step out of author mode for a moment and speak to you personally from one Christian to another and tell you what makes me happy. First, it makes me happy knowing I am a born-again Christian, my salvation was given to me by God, and it is kept secure for me by God. I thank God everyday that this gift of salvation was not obtained by my ability to keep God's laws and is not kept by my ability to live a life without ever sinning. God knows neither I, nor any other Christian, is capable of living a sinless life. It makes me exceedingly happy that I have close fellowship with God, a personal relationship with Him. He is my father and I love Him and I want to live a life that is pleasing to Him. I talk to Him everyday all day throughout the day and He listens to me and He talks back to me. He guides me in my life. He helps me answer tough questions and make hard decisions.

A couple of months ago I had to do my taxes. I normally hire a certified public accountant (CPA) since I own an aviation maintenance business and my taxes can be rather difficult. When I take my taxes to the CPA, I take a downloaded copy of my bookkeeping program and I'm done. Not this time. My computer had crashed, and I lost access to all those bookkeeping records for the last ten years. This year I had to go through all the paper receipts and bank records and credit receipts and so on (you get the idea) by hand. I decided if I was going to do all this by hand anyway, I may as well do the taxes too. When I finished doing everything I could, trying to reduce the tax amount owed, it was not a pretty sight. Now don't get me wrong: I am not anti-government and I believe people should pay their taxes and do their part. "Render unto Caesar that which is Caesar's" (Luke 20:25). I also believe I should pay a fair share and I should take advantage of all the legal avenues Uncle Sam has provided for me to reduce my share as much as possible. I'm not going to get into a political conversation here, but I will just say sometimes it is easier to pay for a political philosophy that I agree with than one that I don't. I wasn't sure if I had done everything right, so I started calling people I knew who dealt with this all the time.

This one fellow, who was a friend of a friend, told me he would help me, so I went through the paperwork and told him everything I had done. He immediately told me if I wanted to fix it I was going to have to change some things. I asked him what I needed to do. In the exemptions and deductions sections, he had me change numbers and put in what he told me to. I did what he told me because he was trying to help me and I didn't want to hurt his feelings, but I knew what I was going to do when he was done. Even while we were still putting in these fake numbers God told me that regardless of what it cost me in the end I couldn't do it. As soon as I got off the phone with the man, I took all those numbers out and filed the taxes with my original numbers. It cost me a significant amount of money to do this, but I'm not sorry I did it. I have a clear conscience, and my relationship with God is good. You cannot out-give God. If you do what He tells you to, He will take care of the rest.

Living for God is simple; you just do right in every situation. There are no decisions to make. Most of the time the word of God is clear about what the right thing to do is. When you don't have a clear answer from the word of God then the Holy Spirit will either be happy about a choice you make or He will be grieved about it; He is not shy about letting you know which. If a decision doesn't feel right, if it will hurt anyone, if it makes you look bad in other people's eyes, if it ruins your testimony, if it makes God look bad, if it offends anyone, then it is probably not the right decision. This isn't that hard to figure out, but it is hard to accept sometimes. It's not an easy thing when God tells you go and sell all you have and follow Him.

It makes me happy knowing what God's will is for me and finally doing what He wants me to do and loving it. A wise man once said if you do what you love for a living you will never have to work a day in your life. I have been working on, and flying, airplanes for forty-seven years, and I've loved it, but the time for this is coming to an end. Now what God wants me to do is to write for Him. I have always loved to write, and I have always enjoyed studying God and His word. I don't know if anyone will ever read a single word of it or if it will ever change any lives or make any difference, but I know this is what God told me to do and so I'm expecting great things. Pray for this work to do mighty things for God and His people. I want all Christians to have happiness in their lives and I believe they can and should.

It makes me happy doing things to help other people, both saved and unsaved. Honestly, when I see a person in need I don't ask them if they are saved or not. If God tells me to help someone I am more than happy to do so. I will warn you however, that you can become so happy in helping others that you put yourself in a bind. Don't make your family suffer or do without to help other people who may not even need the help. Your first responsibility is to provide for your own. Of course, if you have clear guidance from God to give, then by all means you should do so. I don't have any secret solution to knowing who really needs help and who is just trying to rip you off, but I trust God so if He tells me to do it then I do. After that my conscience is clear, I feel good, and it is between the recipient of the gift and God what happens after that. After I give it, it is no longer mine or my concern. I never think about it again.

It makes me happy knowing that "as for me and my house we will serve the Lord" (Joshua 24:15). My wife and I found a big sign at a resale shop that has that verse from Joshua written on it. She hung it up in the house on the wall above the sink in the kitchen. It is visible from nearly every room in the house on the bottom floor. She and I are serious about serving God and doing what He says in our house. If you stand with God who can stand against you? Some people worry about evil spirits in their house. My wife and I have no need to worry about that. God lives in our house, and demons want nothing to do with it. You have the Spirit of God living inside you and you already have victory over the devil, he can't touch you. He can put temptations in front of you that will ruin your life but God always provides an escape. Again it is simple: the escape is to do the right thing. Resist the devil and he will flee.

> Greater is He that is in you, than he that is in the world. (1 John 4:4)

It makes me happy knowing that vengeance belongs to God. Jesus tells us we can't pray to God correctly if we have a grudge against our brother. First, forgive your brother and then come back and ask God for forgiveness for yourself. It is a fact that holding a grudge harms you and you alone. Most of the time the person you are holding the grudge against, the person you are angry with, the person you feel did you wrong, doesn't even know you feel that way. It has been my policy to face situations like this head-on. Paul instructs Christians to talk to this brother with two or three witnesses. But first you should try to resolve it between the two of you before it becomes that big of a problem. If I have a problem with someone, or if I feel that person has a problem with me, I will go straight to that person and confront him or her about it. If you did something to offend someone, be quick to apologize. The Bible says forgive and you shall be forgiven, forgive not and ye shall not be forgiven. If you hold ill feelings for people, whether you feel they did you wrong or they feel you did them wrong, you need to fix it and not keep it to yourself. A grudge kept to yourself will fester and grow into a larger problem. More importantly, if you are in this condition it will rob you of any chance to be happy.

It makes me happy knowing and believing that everything that God allows to happen to me is part of his will for me in my life and I am therefore content with whatever he decides is best for me. If you will trust God enough to turn control of your life over to him and be content with what he decides to do with it, you will find your happiness. Living for God means fewer decisions, less stress, less worry, fewer darts of the flesh that we talked about in the beginning. Let the Holy Spirit have all of you and hold on for the ride of your life. If you don't remember anything else in this book, remember this: happiness is letting God control my life and letting him worry about the consequences.

My sincere desire is that somehow this book will help you figure out what happened to your happy and you will be able to get it back. God has given us so many things to be happy about. He doesn't want us to be sad. He said he came that we might have life and have it more abundantly (John 10:10). God wants you to have a life full of joy as we have seen in so many verses. Please let me know if this book has helped you to find Jesus for the first time or maybe to restore your fellowship with God and reignite your happy. You may send an email to <u>tinbender_dave@yahoo.com</u>.

I pray with thanksgiving
that your joy may be full.
Your humble servant,
David Boudreaux

Printed in the United States
by Baker & Taylor Publisher Services

Printed in the United States
by Baker & Taylor Publisher Services